The
Beach

A History of Virginia Beach, Virginia

Courtesy of the Francis Land House

Queen Anne (1665-1714)

This portrait of Anne, Queen of Great Britain, is attributed to the school of Sir Godfrey Kneller and was painted circa 1710. It features Queen Anne in her coronation robe. The modern day city of Virginia Beach was formed in 1963 from the merger of Princess Anne County (named for her when she was Princess Anne) and the Town of Virginia Beach.

The Beach

A History of Virginia Beach, Virginia

Third Edition
The Virginia Beach Public Library
2006

Cataloging-in-Publication Data

The Beach : a history of Virginia Beach, Virginia / Virginia Beach Public
Library . -- 3rd ed.

    xiv, 161 p. 17 X 25 cm.

    ISBN 0-9779570-0-4

    1. Virginia Beach (Va.)–History. I. Virginia Beach Public Library.

    975.551—dc22

First Edition 1976
Revised Edition , i.e. Second Edition, 1996
Third Edition, 2006

Printed in the United States of America

Cover design by Sue Curcio.

Contents

Reference Map

Many names used in this book refer to places known to local residents but which may not be familiar to others. This reference map gives the reader a basic reference to the geography of Virginia Beach and the major places mentioned in the text.

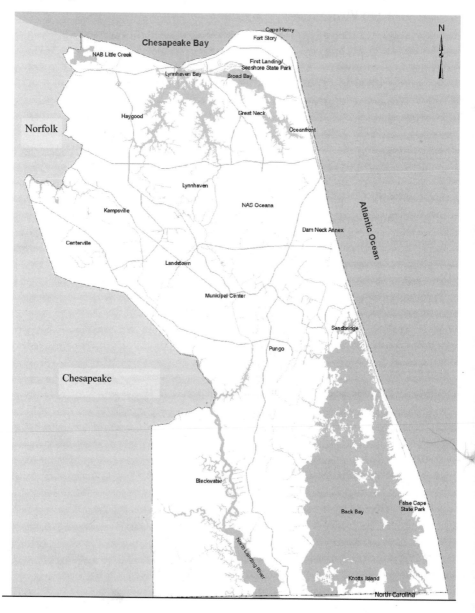

Illustrations

Acknowledgements

First and foremost the 2006 Beach team would like to acknowledge the generous support of The Friends of the Virginia Beach Library. The Friends provided the funding to publish this edition of *The Beach*. We are grateful for all the work that The Friends undertake on behalf of the Library and for their work toward the advancement of a literate populace.

We would like to share our appreciation of all those people and organizations that were mentioned in the Acknowledgements of previous editions of *The Beach*. They are the foundation on which our edition is built.

We thank the following for their permission to use the illustrations in *The Beach*:

Amy Belcher, Virginia Beach Public Library
Jacqueline (Sue) Brown
Albert B. Cain
The Chrysler Museum of Art, Norfolk, Virginia
Peggy Haile-McPhillips, The Norfolk Public Library
Claudia Jew, The Mariners' Museum
Randy Jones, The Virginia Department of Historic Resources
Raymond J. Lewis
The NAS Oceana Public Affairs Office
Carole J. Oste, Public Information Office, The City of Virginia Beach
Deborah Padgett, The Jamestown-Yorktown Foundation
Julie Pouliot, The Old Coast Guard Station
Mark Reed, Historic Resources Coordinator, The Francis Land House
Irene Roughton, The Chrysler Museum of Art
The estate of Charles Sibley
Ruth Hodges Smith, City Clerk, The City of Virginia Beach
Jean Tancredi
The Virginian-Pilot

We particularly wish to acknowledge Robert C. Kennedy, who served as a reader of the manuscript and offered timely and well-thought out advice and suggestions. Any mistakes in grammar, syntax, vocabulary, or clarity of narrative are due to the willfulness of the staff! Thank you, Rob.

Dr. Nathan Altshuler, Professor Emeritus, Anthropology, The College of William and Mary, and his wife Meredith Altshuler, MLS also read and commented on the draft.

Carole J. Oste, Public Information Office, The City of Virginia Beach and Sue Curcio, Media and Communications Office, The City of Virginia Beach, were gracious in taking time to judge the photo contest from which the picture on the cover of *The Beach* was chosen.

Sue Curcio, Creative Designer/Production Coordinator, Media and Communications Department, The City of Virginia Beach designed the cover. Her talent and professionalism are greatly appreciated.

We are thankful that library staff, volunteers, and family responded to our call for photographs. We are pleased to announce that Jean Tancredi's photo won first place and was used on the cover. Albert B. Cain's photograph of the Norwegian Lady was the second place winner and was also used in this edition of *The Beach*.

We wish to acknowledge Susan O'Neill and Nina L. Gilbert, The City of Virginia Beach, ComIT, GIS Mapping who created new maps for this edition of *The Beach*.

We are indebted to Sandy Marshall who planned and executed the Launch Party for *The Beach* and to Mark Reed and the Francis Land House for the venue.

We are especially thankful for library staff Cindy Hart and Susan Marziani who coached us through last minute software glitches and for Felix Rodriguez and Sharla Delancey who provided their expert assistance with our photograph emergencies.

Lastly, we are grateful that the staff of The Virginia Beach Public Library is understanding and willing to accommodate co-workers who are attempting to meet a deadline. For all of the chocolate, encouragement, research, extra time to complete our work, and for being the best of the best, *The Beach* team thanks you.

The Beach Team 2006

Toni Lohman, Team Leader
Mary Lovell Swetnam, Editor and Writer
Alyssa Altshuler, Copy Editor
Booker Bates, Sales and Distribution
Angella Butler, Photo Editor
Theresa G. Dunleavy, Writer
Donna Gant, Marketing and Indexer
Betsy Guglielmo, Design and Layout
Jacqueline S. Lewis, Illustrations and Layout
Nancy Mahone Miller, Production
Sean O'Connell, Indexer
Martha Taylor, Writer
Rita Trammell, Researcher

The Beach Marketing Team 2006

Laura Ashworth
Marcia Hart
Elena Momich

Administrative Support

Lisa Hackett
Susan Marziani
Nancy Moseley
Teresa Shreves

Launch Party

Sandy Marshall

Introduction

In 1995, staff of the Virginia Beach Public Library revised a twenty year old book, *The Beach*. At that time Toni Lohman, Team Leader for *The Beach*, wrote :

> Librarians hesitate to admit they cannot find information, particularly about the history of their own city. This edition of *The Beach* was written because material on the history of Virginia Beach was hard to locate. It was scattered and difficult to use, especially by the students who come to the library every year working on local history projects...

Since that time, several histories and pictorials about Virginia Beach have been published. While they highlight various aspects of life in our city, none of them presents as comprehensive an overview as *The Beach*. By 2006, several circumstances indicated the need for a new edition of *The Beach:* the City of Virginia Beach had continued its evolution as a metropolis rendering parts of the book outdated; there was additional research available for some historic sites; and, the 400th anniversary of the arrival of the first English settlers was fast approaching.

As we celebrate the establishment of the first permanent English colony in the New World, *The Beach* helps us see the continuum from their existence to ours. We still participate in the life of the City through politics, religion, education and recreation. The population has grown from an uneasy cohabitation of English men and Native Americans to a vibrant and exciting blend of ethnicities, languages, and creeds. While some of us may live in high-rises inconceivable to the early settlers, others live or work in their very houses. And even today, we can see at Cape Henry "the white hilly sand like unto the Downes, and along the shores great plenty of Pines and Firres," which Captain John Smith described in 1607.

Chapter 1

Native Virginians

Euacpean explorers and colonists were not the first people to set foot on Virginia's soil. Archaeological evidence indicates that small bands of nomadic hunters had roamed the area for thousands of years prior to the first European encounters with Native Americans.

During the Paleo-Indian period, which ended in 8000 B.C.,[1] local land forms may have been quite different from the present topography of Virginia Beach. Floyd Painter, a local archaeologist, described the ancient Great Neck area as having the highest elevation in lower Tidewater, approximately 200 feet above sea level. The Chesapeake Bay did not exist, except as a broad valley through which the Susquehanna River flowed. The Atlantic shore may have been as much as ninety miles further east than it is today. Paleo-Indian artifacts have been found in the Great Neck, First Landing State Park, and Bayville Farms areas.[2] Archaeologist James G. Pritchard reported uncovering Paleo-Indian fluted point tips, scrapers, and gravers from excavations at the Quail Spring site in the Great Neck area of Virginia Beach.[3]

The climate changed, glacial ice sheets melted, and Paleo-Indian people adapted to their changing environment. As nomadic existence gave way to the use of seasonal habitation sites, the Paleo-Indian period was succeeded by the Archaic period, which dated from approximately 8000 B.C. to 500 B.C. Archaic people left evidence that they revisited their former campsites yearly or seasonally. They hunted, fished, and gathered plants and shellfish. Archaic inhabitants worked with polished stone tools and hunted with a throwing stick, which gave a spear more force. A bannerstone, which was a ground and perforated stone, was attached and may have been used for weight, balance, or supernatural reasons. Bannerstones have been found at Back Bay, Dam Neck, Lynnhaven Inlet and Kempsville.[4]

Archaic people used pots carved out of soapstone. Scientists have used a nuclear reactor and neutron activation analysis to test samples of soapstone in Virginia quarries and compare them with samples taken from prehistoric Indian artifacts and pots. Analysis of the soapstone shows that trading patterns of the tribes were geographical and were specific to language groups. The Chula quarry in Amelia County appears to have been the source of soapstone for most of the Algonquian-speaking Indians, while the Siouan groups used quarries in Albemarle and Nelson Counties.[5]

The term Woodland period categorizes the native people who lived from approximately 1000 B.C. to the European contact period.[6] During this period, the native population increased and village sites became more permanent. Villages were usually located along rivers and creeks, as they were the main routes of transportation and communication. Food gathering and agriculture took precedence over hunting. Indian corn, tobacco, pumpkins, and beans were cultivated. Use of the bow and arrow developed during the Woodland period. In addition to carved bowls, fabric impressed pottery was produced.[7] The Long Creek Midden in the Great Neck Area is an extensive Woodland occupation site.[8]

Courtesy of the Virginia Department of Historic Resources

Virginia Beach Excavation Site, showing original yehakin postholes, circa A.D. 1400 to A.D. 1600
The site was located in a residential neighborhood on Pungo Ridge, north of Great Neck Road. The yehakin on the "Great Neck Site" measured 31 feet long by 16 feet wide.

Courtesy of Jamestown-Yorktown Foundation

Yehakin, scarecrow platform, and garden as created at Powhatan Indian Village, Jamestown Settlement, Williamsburg, Virginia

When Europeans first began exploring the Chesapeake Bay area, Virginia was inhabited by Indians of three linguistic stocks: Iroquoian, Siouan, and Algonquian. The Iroquoian Indians (Nottoway and Meherrin) lived on the south side of the James River. The Siouan tribes (Monacan and Mannahoac) inhabited the area west of the Fall line (the zone typified by river rapids which occur where ground descends from the higher Piedmont elevation to the lower Tidewater areas). The Algonquian tribes occupied the Tidewater area of Virginia, as well as the two Eastern Shore counties of Accomack and Northampton. The Pamlico and Chowanoc peoples, also Algonquian speakers, lived on the Virginia-North Carolina border.

The Chesapeakes, one of the Algonquian tribes, occupied the land from the Atlantic Ocean to the Elizabeth River. They spoke the Powhatan dialect of the Algonquian language, but had initially resisted Powhatan's chiefdom. Powhatan was an Indian chief, who, before the coming of the European colonists, had achieved political dominance over more than thirty Tidewater Algonquian-speaking tribes (having an estimated 14-30,000 members), most of which were conquered or coerced into his confederation. Powhatan inherited authority over the other six tribes —the Powhatan, Arohatock, Appamattuck, Pamunkey, Youghtanund, and Mattaponi. The additional groups were conquered or coerced into joining Powhatan.[9]

The Chesapeakes lived in towns which were named and had boundaries, but which might not be inhabited during all of the seasons. Their dwellings, called *yehakins*, were built of saplings set in the ground in rectangular fashion, bent, and tied together at the top, and covered with bark or mats of reeds and grasses. These mats provided protection from cold winter winds, and could be rolled up to provide ventilation in the summer months. There was a fire pit in the center of the floor and a smoke hole in the roof. A wide shelf around the interior was used for sitting and sleeping. The mats and skins used as bedding could be removed in the daytime and stored. The mats were portable, making village movement possible.[10]

The lodges were usually a short distance apart, and were surrounded by garden plots and fields. The men cleared the fields, and the women planted crops of corn, pumpkins, squash, beans, and tobacco from April to June. They harvested the crops between August and October. The Indians supplemented their winter diet by hunting, gathering, and fishing.

Hunting, by groups or alone, was the men's responsibility. Entire villages would remove to the hunting grounds where deer were captured by various methods. At times, a group of Indian men would form a circle around the deer. The men then set fires around the perimeter of the circle in order to contain the deer. While the deer ran around in the circle seeking a way out, the hunters would shoot them with bows and arrows. A slightly different variation occurred near the rivers. Some hunters would herd the deer toward the river, while others waited in canoes to kill the animals as they swam into the water. At other times, individual hunters would dress in deer skin and antlers and would mimic deer behavior while stalking a deer. When the animal had been wounded by an arrow, the hunter would chase it down until it died. Trapping methods were used for smaller game, such as beaver and otter.[11]

From late March until May, fishing supplied much of the Chesapeakes' diet. Fishing with poles, line, bait, and fishhooks has remained a recognizable method from the time period. However, fishermen would at times leap into the water and swim with the hooked fish until it tired, in order to avoid losing the fish. Fish nets, fish traps, and weirs were used to catch migrating schools of fish. Although there is no archaeological evidence, European drawings of the period show that weirs used by the Powhatan tribe are similar to ones used today.[12] The Chesapeakes supplemented their diet by gathering berries, edible roots, bird eggs. Oysters, clams, and mussels were also important food sources during the late spring and summer.

Although the Chesapeakes were at one time a relatively large tribe, Captain John Smith estimated that there were only 100 warriors in 1607.[13] Near the time that the Jamestown colonists arrived, Powhatan waged a war against the Chesapeakes. Powhatan's priests had prophesied that a nation would rise from the Chesapeake Bay and end his rule. Since the Chesapeakes were the largest tribe on the bay itself, Powhatan assumed that the prophecy referred to them, and he attempted to annihilate them. Through stealth and treachery, he succeeded in killing all the warriors of the tribe, sparing only the women, children, and royal family. The women and children were sent to live among tribes more loyal to Powhatan, mostly in the York River area. Only the royal or ruling family was allowed to stay in the traditional Chesapeake tribal area. Families loyal to Powhatan were sent to replace the dead and deported Chesapeakes. The new families were made subjects of the old Chesapeake royal family, and thus were considered Chesapeakes. These new people may be the ones encountered by John Smith and the other English colonists.[14]

Although full-blooded Chesapeakes are no more, Chesapeake blood may still flow in their Native American, Black, and White descendants. Their name lives on in the great Chesapeake Bay, and in such regional names as the present day City of Chesapeake (to the west of Virginia Beach) and Chesopiean Colony, a residential area in Virginia Beach.

Notes for Chapter 1

1. Duane Champagne, ed., *The Native North American Almanac* (Detroit: Gale Research, Inc., 1994), 3.

2. Floyd Painter, "The Ancient Indian Town of Chesapeake on the Peninsula of Great Neck," *The Chesopiean* 17, August-October 1979, 65.

3. James G. Pritchard, "Quail Spring Paleo Occupation Site," *The Chesopiean* 3, June 1964, 60-61.

4. Ben C. McCary, "Bannerstones from the Dismal Swamp Area and Nearby Counties of Virginia and North Carolina," *Quarterly Bulletin, The Archeological Society of Virginia* 30, September 1975, 36.

5. Beverly Orndorff, "Indian Trading Traced by U.Va. Reactor," *Richmond* (Va) *Times Dispatch*, 12 January 1975, section A, 1.

6. Champagne, 3.

7. Ben C. McCary, *Indians In Seventeenth-Century Virginia* (Charlottesville, Va.: University Press of Virginia, 1957), 93.

8. Edward Jelks, ed. *Historical Dictionary of North American Archeology* (New York: Greenwood Press, 1988), 190.

9. Helen Rountree, *Pocahontas's People: The Powhatan Indians of Virginia through Four Centuries* (Norman, Ok.: University of Oklahoma Press, 1990), 25.

10. Helen Rountree, *The Powhatan Indians of Virginia: Their Traditional Culture* (Norman, Ok.: University of Oklahoma Press, 1989), 60-62.

11. Ibid., 39-40.
12. Ibid., 34-35.
13. Patrick H. Garrow, "An Ethnohistorical Study of the Powhatan Tribes," *The Chesopiean* 12, February - April 1974, 42.
14. Painter, 70-71.

Chapter 2

European Exploration and Settlement

I t is possible, even probable, that European explorers visited the Chesapeake Bay area now called Virginia Beach many years prior to the landing of the Jamestown settlers. There has been a persistent belief that Captain John Cabot may have visited the area in 1498.[1] However, general sources on exploration which mention this notion consider it unlikely.[2] It is also possible that Giovanni da Verazzano sailed past the Virginia capes in 1524. Additionally, there is documentation that in 1546, an English ship rode out a storm in a bay located at the thirty-seventh parallel. This parallel runs through the mouth of the Chesapeake Bay.[3]

In 1570, an expedition of Jesuit priests, a novice, and an Indian guide arrived in Tidewater Virginia and sailed up the James River. They landed on September 10 near what would become Jamestown. The complete tale of this Spanish mission has little impact on the history of Princess Anne County and Virginia Beach, but it helps to illustrate that Europeans were not completely unknown in the area at the time when the "First Landing" occurred.[4]

On April 26, 1607, the vessels *Susan Constant*, *Godspeed*, and *Discovery* arrived in Virginia with 104 Englishmen aboard. Captain George Percy wrote the following account of the landing:

> *The six and twentieth day of April, about four o'clock in the morning, we descried the land of Virginia. . . . The same day we entered into the Bay of Ches-u-pi-oc directly, without any let or hinderance. There we landed and discovered a little way, but we could find nothing worth the speaking of, but fair meadows and goodly tall trees, with such fresh waters running through the woods as I was almost ravished at the first sight thereof.*[5]

This first landing consisted of twenty-eight men who disembarked near what is now Cape Henry. During the night they were attacked by Chesapeake Indians. Captain Gabriel Archer and Mathew Morton, a sailor, were wounded. As the natives disappeared into the woods, the Englishmen retreated to their ships.

On the second day, another party went ashore and penetrated about eight miles inland without encountering any indigenous settlements. This landing was probably east of Lynnhaven Bay (called Morton's Bay after their wounded comrade), as the Chesapeakes' principal town was located near the mouth of the Lynnhaven River. Although no Indians were found, the Englishmen did find a fire where oysters were being roasted. The natives had fled, or at least withdrawn, leaving the oysters in the fire. According to Captain Percy, "We ate some of the oysters which were very large and delicate in taste."[6] These oysters became known as Lynnhaven oysters and enjoyed an international reputation as delicacies into the twentieth century.

On the third day, April 28, 1607, the Englishmen assembled and launched the shallop which they had brought with them. This boat enabled Captain Christopher Newport to take a party northwest on the body of water known, by 1610, as Hampton Roads. Near the present site of Hampton, they saw a forty-five foot Indian dugout log canoe. Inland they reported finding "beautiful strawberries, four times bigger and better than ours in England."[7]

They returned to their anchorage that night, and the following day, April 29, they "set up a cross at Chesapeake Bay, and named that place Cape Henry"[8] in honor of King James's son Henry, Prince of Wales, who was next in line to the throne. Cape Charles, across the bay, was named at the same time for Prince Charles. He later became King Charles I, as his brother Henry died before ascending the throne. Captain John Smith later claimed to have named those headlands himself. However, that is unlikely, as he was under arrest for suspicion of mutiny at the time of his arrival in Virginia.[9] The names were chosen to honor the royal patron of the expedition and his family and to insure their continued interest in colonial pursuits.[10]

The first settlement was planted at Jamestown because the colony was being established as a financial venture by private investors. They were quite clear in their instructions. According to William Strachey (1572-1621), the settlement was not made at Cape Henry or Old Point Comfort (Fort Monroe), because Captain Newport thought that those areas were too exposed. Additionally, the Council (in London) advised that they settle well up into the country, even as much as 100 miles, in order to avoid an attack by the Spanish. The first settlers brought few material possessions with them. They did,

Courtesy of the Chrysler Museum of Art, Norfolk, Virginia

Stephen Reid. ***The Landing at Cape Henry – April 1607***
1928. Oil on canvas, 50" x 62"

Gift of the Organizations and Citizens of Norfolk and vicinity in memory of Alethea Serpell, past President, Council of Assembly Tidewater Women

---

however, bring the English systems of law, local administration, and religion to colonial Virginia.

Once the colony was established, land was granted or patented to adventurers to be settled and civilized. Headrights (land grants consisting of 100 acres per person for arrivals prior to 1616) were given to planters for each person they agreed to transport to Virginia. Because of these patents, the population of colonial Virginia developed into widely separated, self-sufficient, feudal-style manors.

In 1634, administrative units which began as plantations, hundreds, or corporations were grouped into larger areas called shires. The first Virginia shires (or counties) formed were Accawmack, Charles City, Henrico, James City, Warrosquyoake, Charles River, Elizabeth Citty, and Warwick River.[11] The total population of these counties in 1634 was 4,914 people. The area that was to become Princess Anne County was initially part of Elizabeth City (or Citty) County. At its formation in 1634, Elizabeth City extended to both sides of Hampton Roads and contained 1,670 people. Three years later, in 1637, the portion of Elizabeth City County lying south of Hampton Roads became New Norfolk County. The following year, it, in turn, was divided into Upper and Lower Norfolk Counties.[12]

Princess Anne County was formed from the eastern section of Lower Norfolk County in 1691.[13] A small part of the Lynnhaven Parish boundary was erroneously left in Lower Norfolk County until four years later. An act of the assembly of 1695 made Princess Anne County coterminous with the Lynnhaven Parish boundaries, as established in 1642.[14]

Princess Anne County was named for Anne, the younger daughter of James II and Anne Hyde. When King James (II of England and VII of Scotland) was deposed during the "Glorious Revolution" in 1688, his other daughter Mary and her husband, William of Orange, gained the throne. Anne, a staunch Protestant, sided with William in 1688. Mary died in 1694. Following William's death in 1702 Anne became Queen of England. Copies of the document which proclaimed Anne Queen of England, Scotland, France, Ireland, and the Colony Dominion and plantation of Virginia are to be found in various local history sources. The text and punctuation of these documents vary depending on the transcriber. Handwritten and transcribed texts are available on microform, but are difficult to read.

Princess Anne County had a continuous shoreline from the North Carolina-Virginia border, along the Atlantic coast to Cape Henry, and west along the Chesapeake Bay shore to Little Creek Inlet. One look at the map of the area makes it evident why water played an important part in the history of the county. The map is honeycombed with bays, rivers, creeks, and lakes, which reach deep into the county, so that most places were near or had easy access to water. Since water was the colonial means of transportation and communication, nearly every settler had a skiff or shallop for market, church, business, or social activities.

While we consider the Virginia Beach land and water forms we see today to be the same as they were in 1607, it is evident from old maps that several water courses have changed. For instance, Augustin Herrman's map (located in the Library of Congress) shows the inlet for Lynnhaven at Pleasure House Creek about two miles west of the present site. The beginning of the altered inlet is attributed to local fishermen who desired to shorten the circuitous route from the Lynnhaven to their Chesapeake Bay fishing grounds. An 1853 source states that Adam Keeling, Esq. "caused a dike to be cut across from the two nearest or most convenient points on the neighboring shores of the river and bay."[15] The tidal currents gradually eroded the small channel into what is now Lynnhaven Inlet.

A 1695 map of the area (which Sadie Scott Kellam and V. Hope Kellam located in the Library of Congress) indicates that the entire northeast corner of Cape Henry was cut off from the rest of the county by "a continuous water route from Chesapeake Bay in Lynnhaven River, out Long Creek (...'sometimes called Stratton's') into Broad Bay (Battses Bay), into Linkhorn (Lincolne) Bay to Little Neck Creek, or perhaps Chrystal Lake, to the Ocean."[16] There is evidence between Cape Henry and Rudee Inlet of a now non-existent inlet. The maps of the Spanish Jesuit expedition, which explored the Chesapeake Bay in the early fall of 1570, also indicate an inlet near Crystal Lake.[17]

At Lake Tecumseh, also known as Brinson Inlet Lake (per a Virginia Beach Council Resolution dated June 16, 1986), and at Back Bay there are also geophysical indications of harbor inlets. Coastal storms may have changed all of these landmarks just as they continue to change our modern coastline. These waterways throughout the county afforded protection from the sea, provided a means of transportation and communication, and tied the fertile land together.

Notes from Chapter 2

1. Florence Kimberly Turner, *Gateway to the New World: A History of Princess Anne County, Virginia 1607 - 1824* (Easley, S.C.: Southern Historical Press, 1984), 18.
2. Carl Waldman and Alan Wexler, *Who Was Who in World Exploration* (New York: Facts on File, 1992), 110-111.
3. Helen Rountree, *Pocahontas's People: The Powhatan Indians of Virginia through Four Centuries* (Norman, Ok.: University of Oklahoma Press, 1990), 15.
4. Ibid., 16.
5. Conway Whittle Sams, *The Conquest of Virginia: The Second Attempt* (Norfolk, Va.: Keyser-Doherty Printing Corp., 1929), 107.
6. Ibid., 127.
7. Ibid., 129.
8. Ibid., 130.
9. Ibid., 94-95.
10. Ibid., 140.
11. Morgan Poitiaux Robinson, "Virginia Counties: Those Resulting from Virginia Legislation," *Bulletin of the Virginia State Library* 9, nos. 1, 2, 3, January, April, July, 1916, 36.
12. Ibid., 165.
13. William Waller Hening, ed., *The Statutes at Large; Being a Collection of All the Laws of Virginia, from the First Session of the Legislature in the Year 1619* (1819-23; reprint, Charlottesville, Va.: University of Virginia Press for the Jamestown Foundation of the Commonwealth of Virginia, 1969), 95.
14. Ibid., 128.

15. William S. Forrest, *Historical and Descriptive Sketches of Norfolk and Vicinity: Including Portsmouth and the Adjacent Counties, During a Period of Two Hundred Years* (Philadelphia, Pa.: Lindsay and Blakiston, 1853), microfiche, 458.

16. Sadie Scott Kellam and V. Hope Kellam, *Old Houses in Princess Anne Virginia* (Portsmouth, Va.: Printcraft, 1931), 202.

17. Katherine Fountaine Syer, "The Town and City of Virginia Beach," in *The History of Lower Tidewater, Virginia*, vol. 2, ed. Rogers Dey Whichard (New York: Lewis Historical Publishing Company, Inc., 1959), 12.

Chapter 3

Historic Families and Houses

From its founding in 1607 until February 1624/5,[1] an estimated 7,549 people arrived in the Virginia colony. Of these, only one in six (or 1,095) was alive and resident during the 1624/5 muster (a list somewhat like a census).[2] The population was decimated by disease, starvation, returns to England, and Indian attacks. The Massacre of 1622, in which Indians attacked the settlers for 140 miles along the James River, claimed the lives of 350 people.[3]

There was more traveling back and forth between England and the Virginia Colony than might be expected. People sometimes returned to England to stay; however, many times they went to England to conduct business, marry, or to recruit more settlers for the new land. Such recruiting was very lucrative. A headright (a grant of land) was awarded to the person who paid the passage for each individual who entered the colony. Entry by 1616 was worth 100 acres per person and for entry thereafter the award was 50 acres per person.[4]

In June 1624, the Virginia Company charter was dissolved, and the colony became administered by the Crown. A muster, which listed the people and supplies in Virginia, was compiled January 20 through February 7, 1624/5. Persons killed in the 1622 massacre were also listed.[5]

Documentation from the colonial period requires further explanation. For instance, many settlers listed in the muster are noted as "servants." It is suggested that the term "employee" is more apt for the seventeenth century concept than our twenty-first century interpretation of the term "servant."[6] Indentured servants were subject to their masters, but the indenture gave the servant protection under the law. Additionally, spelling was not standardized in the early colonial period. Even proper nouns and names of families varied. Differences occurred according to the ear of the listener, which yielded variations in both vowel and consonant sounds. The same person or members of the same family might use a variety of spellings of the family name during their lifetimes.

Any research into the families that populated the area later known as Princess Anne County reveals a close and sometimes convoluted relationship among them. With so few people living in the colony, it is understandable that the families became intertwined. It was not uncommon for men and women to remarry after the death of a spouse. These tangled relationships seem easier to understand when we examine a few of the families in the young colony.

Families

Families which became mainstays of social, political, and economic life in Princess Anne were among the very first arrivals. The following list (in alphabetical order) gives a flavor of the interrelationships of these early families.

Gookin

Daniel Gookin, who was born in County Kent, England, arrived from Ireland in 1620. He came on his own ship, the *Flying Harte*, and brought eighty people, cattle, and provisions with him. He settled in Newport News at Marie's Mount, which was named for his wife.[7] One son, Daniel, moved from Virginia to Maryland and then Massachusetts for religious reasons. His descendants were closely associated with Harvard College. They married members of the Quincy, Eliot, and Cotton families. [8]

Their other son, John Gookin, was born circa 1613 and probably arrived in Virginia around 1630. In 1636, John acquired 500 acres on the Nansemond River. In the period from 1638 to 1640, he served as a burgess for Upper Norfolk County and a justice for Lower Norfolk County. In 1641 he acquired 640 acres in what became Princess Anne County. In 1640 or 1641, he married Sarah Offley Thorowgood, the widow of his neighbor, Adam Thorowgood.[9] John died November 2, 1643. [10] John and Sarah had a daughter, Mary, who was born in 1642. In adulthood she married Captain William Moseley. After Moseley's death in 1671, she married Lieutenant Colonel Anthony Lawson. Her descendants connected with the Sayer, Thorowgood, Lawson, Moore, Woodhouse,[11] Moseley, Walke, Bassett, and Calvert families.[12]

Offley

Robert Offley was a merchant in London who dealt in goods from Turkey. He was also a member of the Virginia Company, 1609 and a stockholder in the company in 1619. Both his father-in-law and his grandfather-in-law had been Lord Mayor of London.[13] He was deeply involved in the Virginia colony but did not visit it. Two of his daughters, however, married and moved to Virginia. His daughter Sarah married Adam Thorowgood in London in 1627 when she was eighteen. She accompanied him when he returned to Virginia.[14] Following his death in 1640,[15] Sarah married their neighbor Captain John Gookin, who died in 1643. She married Colonel Francis Yeardley in 1647, and he lived until 1655.[16] During their marriages, each husband lived with Sarah at the manor house willed to her by Adam Thorowgood.[17]

Sarah must have been an interesting person, as there are stories still told about her 300 years after her death. One describes a Lower Norfolk court session held at William Shipp's on August 3, 1640. The wife

> of a vestryman made insinuations as to sharp
> business practices on the part of the late Captain
> Thorowgood, where-upon the widow exclaimed,
> "Why, Goody Layton, could you never get
> yours?" (referring to a canceled note which had been
> paid.) The lady flounced around and cried, "Pish!" To
> which Mistress Sarah replied, "You must not think to
> put it off with a 'pish!' for if you have wronged him
> you must answer for it, for though he is dead I am
> here in his behalf to right him." The "goody" was
> required by court order to ask Mistress Sarah's
> forgiveness on her knees, both in Court and on the
> following Sunday in the Parish Church at
> Lynnhaven.[18]

Sarah Offley Thorowgood Gookin Yeardley died in August 1657 at the age of forty-eight. She requested that she be buried next to her second husband, Captain John Gookin.[19] She also requested that her " 'best' diamond necklace" be "sold in England to pay for six diamond rings (probably mourning rings) and two black tombstones, as was indicated in a receipt for an agreement to sell the necklace executed by merchant Nicholas Trott, on February 1, 1657/8."[20] Her armorial tombstone was still visible at Church Point as late as 1819, when its inscription was published in a Richmond newspaper.[21] It read, "Here

lieth ye body of Capt. John Gooking & also ye body of Mrs. Sarah
Yardley who was wife to Captain Adam Thorowgood first, Capt. John
Gooking & Collonel Francis Yardley, who deceased August 1657."[22]
Often, there is not much known about the lives of colonial women;
however, there is a considerable amount of information about Sarah.
She had lived in London and in Virginia, married three influential
men, conducted business in the courts, and was the mother of five
children, who all lived to maturity (four Thorowgood children[23] and
one Gookin child).[24]

Robert Offley had another daughter, Anne, who first married a
Mr. Workman. Her second marriage was to Robert Hayes, who had a
patent of 100 acres on the Lynnhaven River. He had received this
patent for the transportation of the two of them in 1637/8. Robert
Hayes kept the ferry at Little Creek and served as a burgess and
vestryman. In 1643, he patented an additional 750 acres adjoining the
land of his deceased brother-in-law, Captain Adam Thorowgood. The
land patent was granted for the importation of fifteen people,
including the Wortman (Workman) children and his own children,
Alex. and Nathaniel Hayes.[25]

Thorowgood/Thoroughgood

The name commonly spelled as Thoroughgood *was most frequently
spelled* Thorowgood *until the mid-1800s.*

Adam Thorowgood was the seventh son of the vicar of St.
Botolph's Church in Grimston, Norfolk, England. He came to Virginia
on the *Charles* in 1621 and in the 1624/5 muster was listed as
eighteen years old and a "servant" of Mr. Edward Waters of Elizabeth
City.[26] Here is one case where the twenty-first century interpretation
of "servant" seems an unlikely circumstance. Adam Thorowgood was
a member of a large family and although his father was a clergyman,
two of his brothers were Sir Edward and Sir John Thorowgood.[27]
Additionally, in 1626, within two years of being listed as a servant, he
had purchased 150 acres on the north side of Hampton Roads. He left
Virginia sometime after December 1626 and married Sarah Offley in
London the following summer. By 1628, he had returned to Virginia
with his wife, Sarah, and 105 persons for whom he paid passage,
receiving 50 acres per person.[28] He settled on the western bank of the
Lynnhaven River, which was previously called the Chesapeake River.

Adam Thorowgood has traditionally been credited with
associating the name Lynnhaven with this area.[29] His home in
Grimston was about eight miles from King's Lynn in Norfolk County,

England. The name certainly fits the physical description of the area as the term *linn* (or *lynn*) means pool, cascade, or waterfall.[30] The word *haven* means a recess or inlet of the sea, the mouth of a river, a harbor, or a port.[31] The name giver would have known these terms, as they were in common usage at the time.

Adam Thorowgood died in 1640 at the age of thirty-five. His will was probated on April 27 of that year in Quarter Court at James City, rather than in the Lower Norfolk County court. This raises the possibility that he may have died in Jamestown while attending a council session. In view of his position as a council member, probate in the Quarter Court would have been quite natural. Sarah Thorowgood, his wife, was named executrix in his will and inherited, along with a portion of the estate, the Manor House Plantation for life. Their son Adam inherited the rest of his father's houses and lands in Virginia. He would also inherit the Manor House Plantation after Sarah's death. Adam Thorowgood bequeathed 1,000 pounds of tobacco to the Lynnhaven Parish Church to buy "some necessary and decent ornaments" and directed that he be buried in the churchyard at Church Point beside some of his children.[32]

Sarah and Adam Thorowgood's eldest son, Adam, found himself in the midst of a complicated family relationship. In 1646, he married Frances, the daughter of Argoll Yeardley and granddaughter of the former colonial governor, Sir George Yeardley. This meant that his stepfather, Colonial Francis Yeardley, was also his uncle by marriage. Upon his mother Sarah's death in 1657, he came into his complete inheritance and probably moved his wife, Frances, and their family, Argoll, John, Adam III, Francis, Robert, and Rose into the Manor House Plantation, which Sarah had occupied.

When the "Colonel," as he had become known, made his will in 1679, he provided for his wife, Frances, as his father had done for Sarah, by leaving her the Manor House Plantation and 600 acres for life. Upon her death, the plantation would go to his eldest son, Argoll. The remainder of his land and houses were to be divided in five equal parts, one for each of the sons according to their choice in order of seniority. Colonel Adam Thorowgood died in 1685/6.[33] Over the years, the Thorowgood family connected with, among others, the Yeardley, Church, Lawson, Keeling, Nimmo, Woodhouse, Sayer,[34] Custis, Fowke, and Mason families.[35]

Woodhouse

Captain Henry Woodhouse, also from Norfolk County, England, was a member of the Virginia Company, 1609. He served as governor of Bermuda and was from a highly connected family. He was the son of Sir Henry Woodhouse and his wife, Ann Bacon. Ann was the daughter of the Lord Keeper of the Seal and the sister of The Lord Chancellor of England.[36]

Henry Woodhouse (son of Captain Henry and grandson of Sir Henry) patented a headright in 1637 for 500 acres located near the Lynnhaven Inlet. Henry Woodhouse was an attorney and served as justice, burgess, and vestry member.[37] In the generations between their arrival in the colonies and the early 1700s, the Woodhouse family became connected to the Collins, Bennett, Attwood, Keeling, Moore, and Malbone families.[38]

Yeardley

The Yeardley family was also headed by a shareholder of the Virginia Company, 1609. George Yeardley first arrived in Virginia in 1610 following an ill-fated voyage. He had been aboard the *Seaventure* which wrecked in Bermuda as the result of a hurricane. After his belated arrival in Virginia, he became co-commander of Forts Henry and Charles. About 1613, he married Temperence Flowerdew, previously of Norfolk County, England. She had arrived in the colony in 1609. George Yeardley was deputy governor of the colony by 1616. He and Temperence returned to England where they remained until 1618, the year George Yeardley was knighted. He was sent to Virginia as governor and arrived in 1619.[39] During his administration the first representative legislature was convened in the New World.[40] Following his term as governor, the Yeardleys chose to remain in Virginia. In 1626, George was reappointed governor, a position he held until his death in November 1627.

In 1647, one of their sons, Francis, married Sarah Offley, who was the widow of Adam Thorowgood and of John Gookin. Francis's career in politics appears to have been somewhat checkered. He was appointed to the Maryland Council in 1652, but only served a few months. In 1653/4 he had some legal problems, again in Maryland. He was found guilty of illegally seizing a ship and fined 3,000 pounds of tobacco. In the same year, he was charged with "contemptuous carriage and demeanor" toward the Maryland government. Meanwhile, in 1653, he served as a burgess for Lower Norfolk County, and was also a justice. He died in 1656, leaving no children.[41]

Houses

Several of the houses which were built in the early years of Princess Anne County are currently open to the public. Families ranging from ordinary gentry to families of wealth lived in these homes.

Francis Land House
3131 Virginia Beach Boulevard
Owner: City of Virginia Beach

      The Francis Land House is a fine example of the Georgian architectural style that the landed gentry preferred during the second half of the eighteenth century. The house was once thought to have been built in 1732, as there is a brick in the cellar which has those numbers on it. That date is now considered inaccurate. Discussions with the Colonial Williamsburg staff revealed that the construction style of the flooring was not in general use prior to the American Revolution. Also, the interior brickwork in the cellar (three rows of stretchers and one row of headers) [42] was not in common use until

Courtesy of Jean Tancredi, Virginia Beach Public Libraries

Francis Land House, late eighteenth/early nineteenth century construction about 1810.[43] Additionally, in 1992, a dendrochronology analysis, a scientific dating process in which the wood used in construction is dated to its last growing year, was done at the Francis Land House. It indicates that the last year of tree growth was 1804.[44] These items taken together yield a construction date in the late eighteenth/early nineteenth century time frame,[45] with the general consensus being 1805-1810.

The house is built of handmade locally crafted brick laid in Flemish bond.[46] The mortar has a significant content of ground oyster shells. The front door opens into a central passage which, along with the dining room on the right, retains much of its original pine woodwork.[47] The parlor on the left side of the passage is the largest room in the house. A chamber behind the dining room was probably used for sleeping.[48]

The gambrel roof is a distinctive feature and helps to date the house closer to the end of the eighteenth century. The roof was raised approximately twenty inches in 1912, creating a full second story. A brick well remnant has been uncovered behind the house. Twentieth century additions and changes have made the cellar an accessible space.[49]

Six generations of Francis Lands lived on the property from the 1630s until 1819, running a successful plantation with the use of slave labor. In 1819 Francis Moseley Land (the sixth Francis) died, and his personal property was auctioned. However, his daughters, Mary and Ann, inherited his real property. By 1853, neither the house nor the property was owned by Land descendants.[50]

The house was associated with farming operations until the 1950s, when Colin and Mary Studds purchased the building and opened a fashionable dress shop called "Rose Hall."[51] The Francis Land House was purchased by the City of Virginia Beach in 1975[52] and has been open to the public since 1986.

Lynnhaven House
4405 Wishart Road
Owner: Association for the Preservation of Virginia Antiquities

This brick house, on the finger of the Lynnhaven River, was known for many years as the Wishart House or the Boush House. For clarity and due to its proximity to Lynnhaven Bay, it is now called the Lynnhaven House. For many years it was assumed that the Lynnhaven House was built in the mid-to-late 1600s.[53] The scientific dating process, dendrochronology, however, places the house at a much later date. During the process, samples of wood from the floor joists were analyzed.[54] The results indicated that the timbers were cut in the winter of 1724/5.[55] This date suggests that the house was built by Francis Thelaball, who owned the property at that time.

The inventory of Thelaball's estate, taken after his death in 1727, lists furnishings that would have been owned by a man of comfortable, but not wealthy means. There was an absence of prints for the walls, silver, or a list of books. However, the value of the fabric on the beds; enumeration of table linens; a parcel of glass, knives and forks; new and old pewter; and a case of bottles show a level of refinement in the lifestyle enjoyed by the Thelaball family. The estate also listed three boats, cattle, horses, and sheep.[56]

The Lynnhaven House is constructed of brick in the English bond pattern and has two massive gable-end chimneys.[57] It is a story-and-a-half structure with two rooms down and two rooms above. The main door opens directly into the south room (the hall), a multi-purpose room. The north room on the first floor is the kitchen, which contains a very large cooking fireplace. The Lynnhaven House is an

Courtesy of the Virginia Beach Public Library

Lynnhaven House, circa 1725

excellent example of early eighteenth century Tidewater Virginia vernacular architecture.[58] The William W. Oliver, Sr. family presented it as a gift to the Association for the Preservation of Virginia Antiquities in 1971 on the condition that it be restored as an historical monument.[59]

Thoroughgood House
1136 Parish Road
Owner: City of Virginia Beach

Early researchers had assumed that the Thoroughgood House was Captain Adam Thorowgood's Manor Plantation. However, the manor house is now believed to have been situated in the vicinity of Baylake Pines.[60] Current research on the Thoroughgood House suggests that it was built by his son, Argoll (II).[61] The house was remodeled in the early part of the eighteenth century. The interior floor plan was altered slightly and oak panels and wainscoting were installed. The west wall features Flemish bond brickwork and differs from the two gables and east wall, which are of English bond. In 1957, the house was acquired by the Adam Thoroughgood House Foundation, headed by Henry Clay Hofheimer II. It was restored under the direction of Finlay F. Ferguson, Jr., an architect formerly associated with Colonial Williamsburg.[62] During Ferguson's restoration the house faced significant renovation, some of which, according to newer findings, destroyed or hid original aspects of construction.[63]

The Thoroughgood House was acquired in 2003 by The City of Virginia Beach in a creative swap involving the City of Norfolk and the Chrysler Museum.[64] A new study was commissioned to examine the age and historic implications of the site. One of the most intriguing aspects of the new research is the site's connection to the Native American population. According to Floyd Painter, a local archaeologist who conducted excavations at the Thoroughgood House in the 1960s, the site had once been that of a Chesapeake Indian village. The numerous Indian artifacts indicate that it may possibly have been the principal Chesapeake town.[65] Indeed, the possibility that the Adam Thoroughgood House was the site of a Chesapeake Village may be one of its enduring legacies. Despite the significant shifting of the earlier presumed build date of 1680 (or earlier) to 1720, the Thoroughgood House is still a rare survivor of the early colonial period.[66]

Courtesy of Carole J. Oste, Public Information Office, City of Virginia Beach

Adam Thoroughgood House, circa 1680

Upper Wolfsnare
2040 Potters Road
Owner: The Princess Anne County/Virginia Beach Historical Society

The eighteenth century two-story English bond house, with a basement and an attic, stands on land acquired by Thomas Walke III in the 1700s. He probably started building "the brick house" around 1759.[67] Upper Wolfsnare has been essentially restored to its original form. Previously known as the Brick House Farm,[68] or the old Walke Place, it is now known as Upper Wolfsnare. The word "Upper" distinguishes it from Wolfsnare Plantation, which is nearby.

The house was the manor for a plantation of 7,000 acres, much livestock, fifty-five slaves, and a mill. Although plain, it was built with the finest materials. The house has corner fireplaces which are shared between two rooms. Especially noteworthy is its fine woodwork, particularly in the wide central hall.[69]

Thomas Walke IV inherited the house from his father and was residing there in 1788 when he served as one of Princess Anne County's two elected delegates to the Virginia Convention, at which the state ratified the United States Constitution.[70] Thomas Walke IV died childless and the house changed hands many times. Various members of the Boush, Cornick, Ferebee, Fentress, Worrell, and Malbon families (among others) owned the house.

In 1964, the Commonwealth of Virginia purchased the house to insure a right-of-way for the Norfolk-Virginia Beach Expressway (now Route 264). The state had planned to demolish Upper Wolfsnare and use the land for fill during the road project. An agreement was reached between the highway department and the Princess Anne Historical Society, which enabled a land trade to save the house. Mr. and Mrs. James Sadler owned adjacent land that was used as road fill, thus saving Upper Wolfsnare. The Upper Wolfsnare property was deeded to the Princess Anne Historical Society.[71]

An archaeological dig took place on the site in 1979. Because the area had been lived on and farmed for hundreds of years, there were few remaining early artifacts. However, portions of Chinese export porcelain, fine pearl wares, case bottles, and a wine bottle seal were found. These all indicate that a family of some substance lived in the house between 1760 and the early 1800s.[72]

Notes from Chapter 3

1. Dates listed with a slash indicate both the Julian and the Gregorian years. The dates concerned are between January 1 and March 25 (the Julian New Year) until the year 1752 when the calendars were consolidated. For instance, 20 February 1652/3 meant that the date was 1652 in the Julian calendar and 1653 on the Gregorian calendar.
2. Virginius Dabney, *Virginia, the New Dominion* (Charlottesville, Va.: University Press of Virginia, 1982), 36.
3. Ibid., 35.
4. Virginia M. Meyer and John Frederick Dorman, eds., *Adventurers of Purse and Person: Virginia 1607-1624/5*, 3rd ed., (Richmond, Va.: Dietz Press, Inc., 1987), xxvi.
5. Ibid., 3.
6. Ibid., xxviii.
7. Ibid., 311-312.
8. Ibid., 316-318.
9. Ibid., 314.
10. "Gookin Family," in *Genealogies of Virginia Families from the Virginia Magazine of History and Biography*, vol. 5, Randolph-Zouch (Baltimore, Md.: Genealogical Publishing Co., Inc., 1981), 690.
11. Meyer and Dorman, eds., 318-319.
12. "Gookin Family," 691.
13. Meyer and Dorman, eds., 459.
14. Ibid., 460.
15. Ibid., 608.
16. Ibid., 727.
17. Rogers Dey Whichard, *The History of Lower Tidewater Virginia*, vol. 1 (New York: Lewis Historical Publishing Company, Inc., 1959), 263.
18. Ibid., 266.
19. George Carrington Mason, *Colonial Churches of Tidewater Virginia* (Richmond, Va.: Whittet and Shepperson, 1945), 132.
20. Whichard, vol. 1, 275.
21. Mason, 132.
22. Whichard, vol. 1, 253.
23. Meyer and Dorman, eds., 609.
24. Ibid., 315.
25. Ibid., 459-460.
26. Ibid., 608.

27. "Thoroughgood Family," in *Genealogies of Virginia Families from the Virginia Magazine of History and Biography*, vol. 5, Randolph-Zouch (Baltimore, Md.: Genealogical Publishing Co., Inc., 1981), 482.

28. Meyer and Dorman, eds., 608-609.

29. Mason, 128.

30. *Oxford English Dictionary*, 2nd ed., s.v. "linn."

31. Ibid., s.v. "haven."

32. Whichard, vol. 1, 262-263.

33. Ibid., 264.

34. "Thoroughgood Family," 482.

35. Meyer and Dorman, eds., 699.

36. Ibid., 699.

37. Ibid., 700.

38. Ibid., 699-703.

39. Ibid., 724-725.

40. "George Yeardley," in *Genealogies of Virginia Families from the Virginia Magazine of History and Biography*, vol. 5, Randolph-Zouch (Baltimore Md.: Genealogical Publishing Co., Inc., 1981), 918.

41. Meyer and Dorman, eds., 727.

42. A stretcher is the long side of a brick and a header is the short end of a brick. Brickwork patterns and styles have changed over time and can be useful in dating a structure.

43. Mark Reed, letter to the author, 24 April 1996.

44. Herman J. Heikkenen, *The Last Year of Tree Growth for Selected Timbers within the Francis Land House as Derived by Key-Year Dendrochronology* (Blacksburg, Va.: Dendrochronology, Inc., 1992).

45. Mark Reed, 24 April 1996.

46. Flemish bond is a pattern in which brick was laid. Stretchers (the long side of the brick) were laid in an alternating pattern with headers (the short end of the brick) in the same horizontal row. Vertically, the stretchers were placed over the headers in the lower row. This pattern is said to have become popular after the 1666 Great Fire of London. English bond refers to a pattern of brickwork where stretchers and headers make up individual rows which are laid in an alternating pattern vertically, stretchers upon headers.

47. City of Virginia Beach, Va. The Office of Research and Strategic Analysis. *City of Virginia Beach Inventory of Historic Buildings and Sites* (Virginia Beach, Va.: City of Virginia Beach, 1990), March 1990, 4-13.

48. Mark Reed, letter to the author, 13 April 1996.

49. Ibid.

50. Mark Reed, 24 April 1996.

51. Mark Reed, 13 April 1996.

52. Bert Rohrer, "Beach Council Okays Purchase of Rose Hall," *Virginian-Pilot*, 17 June 1975, section A, 3.

53. Mary Reid Barrow, "No Historical Lies," *Virginia Beach Beacon*, 1 July 1983, 22.

54. Mary Reid Barrow, "Lynnhaven House has a Burgeoning Past," *Virginia Beach Beacon*, 16 February 1986, 6.

55. Herman John Heikkenen, *Final Report: The Year of Construction of the Lynnhaven House as Derived by Key-year Dendrochronology Technique* (Blacksburg, Va.: The American Institute of Dendrochronology, 1982).

56. *Princess Anne County Will Book*, 1724-1735, 129.

57. Betty Pettinger, "17th Century House Called One of the Best Preserved in the U.S.," *Richmond* (Va.) *Times Dispatch*, 4 September 1974, section A, 8.

58. Marilyn S. Melchor, letter to the author, April 1996.

59. City of Virginia Beach, Va. The Office of Research and Strategic Analysis, March 1990, 4-13.

60. Florence Kimberly Turner, *Gateway to the New World: A History of Princess Anne County, Virginia, 1609-1824* (Easley, S.C.: Southern Historical Press, 1985), 35.

61. Nicholas M. Luccketti, "Archaeological Assessment of the Adam Thoroughgood House Site, Virginia Beach, Virginia," (Draft document) (Williamsburg, Va.: James River Institute for Archaeology, Inc., December 13, 2005), 53.

62. Joanne Young, "Brick House Here Believed Oldest in America to be Dedicated Monday; Restoration Complete," *Virginian-Pilot*, 27 April 1957, 7

63. Willie Graham and Carly Carlson, "Archaeological Assessment of the Adam Thoroughgood House Site, Virginia Beach, Virginia" (Draft document) (Williamsburg, Va.: James River Institute for Archaeology, Inc., December 13, 2005),14.

64. "Beach Gift to Chrysler a Coup for Local History," *Virginian-Pilot*, 8 May 2003, B10.

65. Floyd Painter, "Artifacts from the Thoroughgood Site," *The Chesopian*, 3, December 1965, 130.

66. Nicholas M. Luccketti, "Archaeological Assessment of the Adam Thoroughgood House Site, Virginia Beach, Virginia" (Draft document) (Williamsburg, Va.: James River Institute for Archaeology, Inc., December 13, 2005), 55.

67. Stephen S. Mansfield, *Princess Anne County and Virginia Beach: A Pictorial History* (Virginia Beach, Va.: The Donning Company/Publishers, 1989), 35.

68. Sadie Scott Kellam and V. Hope Kellam, *Old Houses in Princess Anne Virginia* (Portsmouth, Va.: Printcraft, 1931), 195.

69. City of Virginia Beach, Va. The Office of Research and Strategic Analysis, March 1990, 4-13.

70. Mansfield, 214.

71. Louisa Venable Kyle, "Upper Wolf Snare Plantation" (typescript, 1971).
72. Andrew C. Edwards and Norman F. Barka, *The Archaeology of Upper Wolfsnare, Virginia Beach, Virginia* (Williamsburg, Va.: The College of William and Mary, 1979), vi-vii.

Chapter 4

Witches and Witchcraft

While colonial history tends to focus on the witch trials in Salem, Massachusetts, numerous trials were also held in Princess Anne County, Virginia. Apparently malicious accusations were a problem because in a 1655 Lower Norfolk County court order stated that anyone making an accusation of witchcraft was liable for a fine, and a possible censure by the court, if he were unable to prove his charge under oath and with witnesses.[1] In December 1659, the court enforced its ruling by fining Thomas Godby 300 pounds of tobacco, along with court costs of twenty pounds of tobacco, because his wife, Ann, made an unsubstantiated accusation of witchcraft against Mrs. Nicholas Robinson.[2] Accusations could include the sickening of people or animals, prophetic utterences, riding on people or animals, flying through the air or bewitching animals, people or crops.

Nearly twenty years passed before the county court recorded John Samon's accusation against Alice Cartwrite concerning the death of his child, whom Alice was said to have bewitched. An all-female jury searched Alice's body for marks indicative of the occult. Finding none, they acquitted her.[3]

On July 8, 1698, John and Anne Byrd were the plaintiffs in two separate defamation suits. Charles Kinsey had accused Anne of being a witch and testified that she had ridden him from his house. That same day the Byrds again appeared in court, suing John Pitt for accusing them of being in league with the devil. Pitt claimed that the Byrds had ridden him along the seashore to his home. The Byrds lost both suits.[4] Although these suits are hardly what one associates with witchcraft trials, they were the forerunners of the trials of Grace Sherwood, popularly known as the "Witch of Pungo."

Beginning in February 1697, there were a series of suits for slander initiated by Grace and James Sherwood against Richard Capps, John and Jane Gisburne, and Anthony and Elizabeth Barnes. These people had previously accused the Sherwoods of witchcraft. The suit against Capps was amicably settled and dismissed. However, the Gisburnes insisted that Grace had bewitched their cotton. The Barneses contended that Grace had come to Elizabeth in the night, ridden her, and "gone out of the Key hole or crack of the door like a black Catt."[5] These trials lasted four days, with the same all-male jury impaneled for both suits. The fact that both verdicts were against the Sherwoods seems to have been indicative of future judgements.[6]

In 1701, James Sherwood died and Grace became the administratrix of his small estate. Four years later, court records show that Grace sued Luke Hill and his wife for trespassing, assault, and battery. Grace was awarded only twenty shillings and court costs. Mark Powell, the jury foreman, neglected to sign the verdict, so the judgment had to be carried over until the next term.[7] Powell had previously been a juror in the 1698 suits of the Sherwoods against the Gisburnes and the Barneses.[8]

On February 6, 1705, the Hills made a formal complaint against Grace on suspicion of witchcraft. The following March, the court summoned a jury of women to search Grace's person for any telltale marks indicative of a witch. It is not surprising that their

July 10th 1706

Whearas Grace Sherwood being Suspected of witchcraft have a long time waited for a ffit uppertunity ffor a further Examination and by her Consent & approbacon of ye Court it is ordr yt ye Sherr take all Such Convenient assistance of boate & men as Shall be by him thought ffi8t to meet at Jno Harpers plantacon in ordr to take ye Sd Grace forth with & but her into above mans Debth and try her how She Swims Therein alwayes having Care of her life to p'serve her from Drowning & as Soon as She Comes Out yt he request as many Ansient & knowing women as possible he Cann to Serch her Carefully ffor all teats spots & marks about her body not usuall in Others & yt as they ffind ye Same to make report on Oath To ye truth thereof to ye Court & further it is ordr yt Som women be requested to Shift & Serch her before she goe into ye water yt She Carry nothing about her to cause any further Suspicion.

The Lower Norfolk County Virginia Antiquary, NY: Peter Smith, 1951, vol. 3, p. 36

Transcribed Court Order

Courtesy of the Old Coast Guard Station and Charles Sibley

Charles Sibley. (1921-2005) ***Witch Ducking in 1706, Grace Sherwood***

search was successful, since the forewoman of the jury was the same Elizabeth Barnes who had been the defendant in previous litigation involving the Sherwoods.[9]

Though the jury claimed to have found marks on Grace, the court was apprehensive about passing judgment. Luke Hill appealed to the attorney general, Stephen Thompson, in Williamsburg. This higher court refused to hear the case because it was too general and did not charge Grace with a particular act. The case was returned to the jurisdiction of the county. More hearings were held during the next several months, and finally in July 1706, Grace consented to a trial by ducking. Scheduled for July 5, the ducking was postponed until Wednesday, July 10, due to inclement weather.[10]

On that day, Grace was brought to John Harper's plantation on the Lynnhaven River. She was tied in the manner customary for ducking, her right thumb to her left toe and her left thumb to her right toe, and cast into the river. It was believed that a witch would not sink, and Grace managed to stay afloat. The crowd of spectators, and the women designated to search her after the ordeal, judged her to be a witch. The sheriff took her into custody for future trial. She was imprisoned in the county jail, but eventually released. There is no evidence that any further action was taken against her.[11]

Over the years Grace Sherwood, the alleged "Witch of Pungo," has become the subject of many local legends. At her ducking, she is said to have told the spectators, "not one of ye will see me ducked. But I'll see all of ye ducked."[12] The day was beautifully clear, but just as she was taken out of the water, a terrible storm came up. The fury of the thunder, lightning, and rain sent the crowd into a panic, while Grace stood by calmly watching.[13]

It is said that one night Grace needed some rosemary. Discovering that a ship was anchored off Lynnhaven Town, she sailed to it in an eggshell and bewitched the cabin boy. She then summoned a strong wind, sailed the ship to England, and returned the same night with a sprig of rosemary. Legend has it that the rosemary bushes in Princess Anne County came from the sprig that Grace brought back from England. It is also told that once, while she was waiting to be hanged, Grace asked a boy to bring her two unwashed pewter plates. When he handed the plates to her, she put one under each arm and promptly flew off across Currituck Sound, escaping her execution.[14]

One of the strangest legends concerning Grace is said to have taken place at her death in 1740.[15] As she lay ill during a fierce storm, Grace asked her sons to move her from her bed and place her feet into the warm ashes of the fireplace. During the night a tremendous gust of wind came down the chimney, scattering embers everywhere. When Grace's sons looked in on her, they discovered that she had disappeared. All that remained of their mother was the imprint of a cloven hoof in the ashes.[16] Such tales were told to generations of children in Princess Anne County. Public perception changes over time. These stories became less credible in the modern era. A bronze statue of Grace has been designed and fundraising for the $90,000 needed has begun. Plans call for the completed statute to be placed near where Grace Sherwood was tried in July 1706.[17]

Notes for Chapter 4

1. Benjamin Dey White, "Gleanings in the History of Princess Anne County," in *An Economic and Social Survey of Princess Anne County* (Charlottesville, Va.: Michie Company, 1924), 13.

2. Edward W. James, *The Lower Norfolk County Virginia Antiquary*, vol. IV, (New York: Peter Smith, 1951), 36.

3. Ibid., vol. I, 56-57.

4. Ibid., vol. I, 20-21.

5. Ibid., vol. II, 93.

6. Ibid., vol. II, 92-93.

7. Ibid., vol. II, 139-140.

8. Ibid., vol. II, 93.

9. Ibid., vol. II, 140-141.

10. Ibid., vol. III, 35-36.

11. George Holbert Tucker, "Grace Sherwood of History and Legend: Princess Ann's (sic) Double Witch," *Norfolk Virginian-Pilot*, 13 November 1949, Part 5, 1.

12. W.H.T. Squires, *The Days of Yester-Year in Colony and Commonwealth* (Portsmouth, Va.: Printcraft Press, Inc., 1928), 74.

13. Ibid.

14. Agnes White Thomas, "Princess Anne's Own: Meet Grace Sherwood – A Genuine Witch," *Virginian-Pilot and the Portsmouth Star*, 28 April 1957, section E, 1.

15. George H. Tucker, "Tidewater Landfalls: Devil in Princess Anne," *Virginian-Pilot*, 23 July 1959, 25.

16. Tucker, "Grace Sherwood of History and Legend," 11.

17. "Grace Sherwood Statue," Ferry Plantation House, (Virginia Beach, n.d.)

Chapter 5

Pirates

From the earliest days of the European settlements in the New World, piracy flourished in the coastal waters of North America.[1] When Sir Francis Wyatt arrived in Virginia to be governor in 1621, he came with numerous instructions from the Crown on its governance. Of primary importance was his instruction to punish pirates and to build fortresses for the defense of the colony.[2]

According to historian Hugh E. Rankin, the golden age of piracy began about 1630 in Tortuga, Spain with the formation of the "Confederacy of the Brethren of the Coast," a pirate "republic."[3] During this golden age of piracy, there was extensive trade between the newly formed colonies in the Americas and their home countries in Europe. Due to the great distances involved and the unfamiliarity with unknown waters, policing the coast of the colonies was very difficult, leaving many merchant ships vulnerable to attack by pirates and other hostile vessels.[4]

During the seventeenth century, Spain, England, Holland, and France, warred with one another frequently. The warring nations would license privateers to attack and loot an enemy's ships. When peace was declared, many privateers, unwilling to abandon lucrative careers, turned to piracy.[5]

The rich commerce of Virginia made the cargo-laden vessels of the Chesapeake Bay tempting targets for pirates. Forts had been established in the colony for protection, but by 1691 most of Virginia's forts were in very poor condition. Land fortifications were not a sufficient safeguard from pirates and privateers, so Virginia turned to guardships from England for protection.[6] Because of the threat of pirate attack, merchant ships were ordered to assemble at a given point in the Chesapeake Bay (often Point Comfort or Lynnhaven Bay) and sail in convoy under the protection of a guardship.[7]

In July of 1699, the waters of Lynnhaven Bay were terrorized by a pirate ship, the *Alexander* (originally named *Providence Frigate* and also known as *Providence Galley*),[8] commanded by John James.

Having learned of the vulnerability of Virginia's naval defenses from record books taken from a captured ship, James saw his opportunity to plunder Virginia's waters with impunity. The Virginia guardship *Essex Prize*, commanded by Captain John Aldred, engaged the pirate ship in battle, but being outgunned and undermanned, the guardship withdrew. The *Alexander* went on to loot two merchant ships, *Maryland Merchant* and *Roanoke Merchant*, and then left the area unhindered.[9]

Virginia's government was greatly alarmed by these attacks and was also concerned about possible pirate landings. The need for a larger, more powerful guardship was apparent, and Governor Sir Francis Nicholson appealed to the king for help.[10] The governor also ordered the militias in the counties of Norfolk, Princess Anne, Accomack, Northampton, and Elizabeth City to post lookouts to patrol the shores, looking for strange or suspicious sails. One such lookout patrolled the beach between Cape Henry and Lynnhaven River.[11]

In April 1700, the French pirate ship *La Paix*, commanded by Frenchman Louis Guittar, practically brought shipping in Virginia to a halt. After taking a number of vessels near the capes, Guittar sailed into Lynnhaven Bay and began plundering vessels anchored there.[12] Edward Whittaker was the master of the *Indian King*, a ship that Guittar had plundered outside the capes. Guittar questioned Whittaker about the threat of guardships in Virginia's waters. Whittaker told him about the *Essex Prize*, a sixth-rater, which he believed had returned to England.[13] (British warships were rated according to the number of guns they carried. There were six rates, with first-rate being the most powerful, sixth-rate being the least. First-rate ships carried 100 guns or more, sixth-raters carried up to 32.[14] The *Essex Prize* had only 16 guns.)[15] Feeling safe from the threat of colonial guardships, *La Paix* went on to plunder nine ships whose combined cargo was valued at £20,000.[16]

Unbeknownst to Guittar, the British man-of-war *Shoreham*, commanded by Captain William Passenger, had arrived to replace the *Essex Prize*. Alerted to the presence of the pirate ship by a small vessel on its way down the Chesapeake Bay, Governor Nicholson ordered the *Shoreham* to set sail to engage *La Paix*. Governor Nicholson and Captain Aldred were also aboard the *Shoreham*.[17] After ten hours of fierce fighting, the pirate ship ran aground at Lynnhaven and was forced to strike her colors and surrender.[18] Captain Guittar and sixty-four of his pirate crew were sent to England in chains where they were tried and convicted. On November 23, 1700, Guittar and twenty-three of his companions were hanged. Soon afterwards, forty others met the same fate.[19]

Three members of the pirate crew, however, were not on board *La Paix* when she surrendered and so were not included in the Articles of Capitulation. John Houghling, the pilot, had jumped overboard and was apprehended near Lynnhaven after swimming ashore. Cornelius Franc and Francois Delaunee were aboard the previously captured merchant vessels when *La Paix* surrendered. All three were tried in a special Court of Admiralty in Elizabeth City. They were convicted and it was ordered that they be turned over to the custody of Sheriff Major John Thorowgood of Princess Anne County for execution. They escaped to Accomack but were recaptured and returned to Princess Anne County, where they were hanged in chains.[20]

Unfortunately, the capture of *La Paix's* crew did not herald the end of piracy in Virginia. During the early part of the eighteenth century, Virginia and North Carolina were victimized by the notorious pirate Blackbeard. Although his identity is obscure, it is generally accepted that Blackbeard was Edward Teach, a seaman from Bristol, England.

During the reign of Queen Anne, Blackbeard was a privateer, attacking and looting only the enemies of the queen. When peace came to England in 1713, he turned to piracy. He captured a French merchant ship, outfitted her with forty cannons, renamed her *Queen Anne's Revenge*, and preyed on colonial commerce.[21]

Blackbeard was granted the king's pardon from North Carolina's governor Charles Eden, who was intimidated by Blackbeard and lacked the ability to confront his ruthless acts of piracy.[22] Blackbeard took up residence in Bath, North Carolina, becoming a local celebrity. He was able to plunder with immunity and made the shallow sounds of North Carolina's Outer Banks his base of operations. From here, the trade-rich waters of Virginia to the north were an easy mark, as were the waters of Charleston to the south.[23]

Locally, legends of Blackbeard and his buried treasure abound. There is an island in Lake Joyce that is now known as Blackbeard's Island. It is an old breastwork, or fort, and was at one time called Pirate's Fort. Tradition has it that this island was created by pirates. According to W. H. T. Squires in *The Days of Yester-Year in Colony and Commonwealth*, "the firm land originally thrust a point into the calm and clear waters of the bay, in the shape of the letter V. The pirates dug a canal across the little cape which made it an islet, a no mean labor for the canal is approximately twenty-five feet wide."[24] The excavated soil was thrown up on the island side creating an artificial hill. It was believed that pirate sentinels watched vessels entering Virginia's capes from this location. Even after two-and-a half centuries of erosion, this hill remains a prominent elevation, rising about twenty feet above the canal.

Historians believe that Lake Joyce was once part of a continuous waterway from Little Creek to Lynnhaven.[25] Years ago there was an inlet to the bay through these waters. The present inlet, two miles further east, was dug to shorten the route for small boats to the Chesapeake Bay. Over time the egress from Lake Joyce was blocked by shifting sands, so it no longer provides access to Lynnhaven Bay.

At one time, it was possible to stand at the summit of Pirate's Fort and see Cape Henry four miles to the east. Blackbeard's Hill, one of the highest dunes of Cape Henry (fifty feet above sea level), could also be seen. According to Squires, "A sentinel on Blackbeard's Hill could easily detect a merchantman miles away, signal the crew at Pirate's Fort, and Blackbeard would be ready, armed and waiting long before his unsuspecting victim had turned into the channel at Cape Henry."[26]

Today, Blackbeard's Island is privately owned. The view from the island to the east is blocked by dense foliage and by the construction of houses in the area. The exact location of what was called Blackbeard's Hill is now unknown. However, in First Landing State Park on the south side of Shore Drive, there exists an ancient sand dune which rises about eighty feet above sea level. The sand dunes are forested now, but in winter when the leaves are gone, one can still see the waters of Virginia's capes and all the ships entering and leaving there.[27]

Blackbeard was a ruthless and cruel man. He once shot one of his own crewmen in the knee, crippling him for life, as a lesson to his crew.[28] He not only threatened merchant ships but also victimized citizens on shore, robbing, plundering, and looting at will. With the immunity under which Blackbeard and other pirates acted in North Carolina, there was a real fear that Ocracoke Island would be turned into a pirate enclave.[29]

The treachery of Blackbeard and his pirate band was so devastating that the North Carolina settlers along Albemarle and Pamlico Sounds clandestinely appealed to Virginia's governor,

Death of Black Beard.

Courtesy of the Mariners' Museum, Newport News, Virginia

Death of Blackbeard
Blackbeard meets his demise on board the *Jane*, the ship of British Navy
Lieutenant Robert Maynard.

Alexander Spotswood, for help. The governor, who had arrived in Virginia in 1710, was committed to the eradication of piracy in Virginia's waters and was tireless in his pursuit of punishment for convicted pirates.[30] Fearing that Virginia's waters would suffer a fate similar to North Carolina, he resolved to put an end to Blackbeard.[31]

Governor Spotswood's actions against Blackbeard were carried out in great secrecy. There were two reasons for this. First, Spotswood did not want Blackbeard to be forewarned and escape. Second, sending armed forces into Governor Eden's jurisdiction was an affront to Eden's authority. At his own expense, Spotswood hired two sloops to track Blackbeard down. He also convinced the government of Virginia to offer a £100 reward for Edward Teach, dead or alive.[32]

Lieutenant Robert Maynard set sail from Kecoughtan (now Hampton) on November 17, 1718. On the morning of November 21, Maynard discovered Blackbeard's two pirate sloops lying at anchor in a sheltered cove in Ocracoke Inlet. The next day a terrible battle took place. Coming alongside Maynard's vessel, the *Jane*, Blackbeard and several of his crew boarded the ship and the fighting was hand-to-hand. Maynard and Blackbeard engaged in a life and death struggle. When the fighting ended, the decks were littered with the dead and dying.

Blackbeard was killed that day, sustaining no less than twenty-five cut wounds and five pistol shots.[33] "Hardly had the smoke from the battle cleared, and the moans of the wounded and dying still heavy in the air, than those who remained jubilantly severed Blackbeard's head from his body and hung it from the bowsprit of *Jane*".[34] In Lloyd Haynes Williams's account he says, "According to tradition, the head dangled for many years from a pole at the mouth of the Hampton River near Kiquotan as a warning to mariners and this place is known even today as Blackbeard's Point."[35]

Fifteen surviving members of Blackbeard's crew were taken to Williamsburg where they were tried by a Court of Admiralty for piracy. Thirteen were convicted and hanged.[36] Though piracy in Virginia's waters did not end with Blackbeard's death, it was in a rapid decline. By the late 1720s, the golden age of piracy was over.

Queen Anne's Revenge ran aground and was lost at Beaufort Inlet in June, 1718. In 1996, divers from a shipwreck salvage company, Intersal, Inc., discovered a shipwreck at Beaufort Inlet,

North Carolina, that many experts believe is Blackbeard's flagship, the *Queen Anne's Revenge*. Artifacts recovered from the site provide strong evidence for their claims.[37]

Efforts to identify the shipwreck found as Blackbeard's flagship is the work of The QAR Project, a joint venture of the North Carolina Department of Cultural Resources, Division of Archives and History, Underwater Archaeology Branch, and Maritime Research Institute, a non-profit arm of Intersal. Together with marine archaeologists and other scientists from around the world, they are studying the wreck and its artifacts. Many of the artifacts are on view for public display in the North Carolina Maritime Museum in Beaufort, North Carolina.

Notes for Chapter 5

1. Hugh F. Rankin, *The Golden Age of Piracy* (Williamsburg, Va.: Colonial Williamsburg, 1969), 1.
2. Donald G. Shomette, *Pirates on the Chesapeake* (Centreville, Md.: Tidewater Publishers, 1985), 7.
3. Rankin, 8-9.
4. Lloyd Haynes Williams, *Pirates of Colonial Virginia* (Richmond, Va.: Dietz Press, 1937), 21-22.
5. Nancy Roberts, *Blackbeard and Other Pirates of the Atlantic Coast* (Winston Salem, N.C.: John F. Blair, Publisher, 1993), xii.
6. Williams, 4-5.
7. Ibid., 7.
8. Shomette, 104.
9. Ibid., 104-110.
10. Ibid., 111.
11. Williams, 51.
12. Ibid., 53.
13. Ibid., 57.
14. Peter Kemp, ed., The *Oxford Companion to Ships and the Sea* (New York: Oxford University Press, 1976), 692.
15. Shomette, 105.
16. Williams, 53.
17. Ibid., 58-59.
18. Robert Beverley, *The History and Present State of Virginia* (Chapel Hill, N.C.: University of North Carolina Press, 1947), 110.
19. Shomette, 150-151.
20. Ibid., 149.
21. W. H. T. Squires, *The Days of Yester-Year in Colony and Commonwealth: A Sketch Book of Virginia* (Portsmouth, Va.: Printcraft Press, Inc., 1928), 50.
22. Shomette, 198-199.
23. Squires, 51.
24. Ibid., 52.
25. Katherine Fontaine Syer, "The County of Princess Anne, 1691-1957," in *The History of Lower Tidewater, Virginia*, vol. 2, ed. Rogers Dey Whichard (New York: Lewis Historical Publishing Company, Inc., 1959), 54.
26. Squires, 54.
27. Philip J. Roehrs, Coastal Engineer, City of Virginia Beach Public Works, Office of Beach Management, telephone interview by author, Virginia Beach, Va., 4 January 1996.
28. Shomette, 203.
29. Ibid., 205.
30. Ibid., 204-216.
31. Ibid., 208.
32. Ibid., 210.
33. Ibid., 214.
34. Ibid., 215.

35. Williams, 113.
36. Shomette, 216.
37. Constance Bond, "A Fury from Hell or Was He?," *Smithsonian*, 30, no.11 (Feb. 2000), 62-72, http://search.epnet.com.

Chapter 6

Cape Henry, First Landing State Park, and the Lighthouses

Cape Henry, the site of the first lighthouse erected by the United States government,[1] has contributed significantly to the history of Virginia Beach. At one time the cape was a sand island, stretching from Stratton's Creek to the Lynnhaven River. Eventually this island became part of the mainland, making up the entire northeast corner of what is now Virginia Beach.

Early sources refer to Cape Henry as "the Desert," a term which is actually misleading. The cape was not made up of desert terrain, but was simply an uninhabited stretch of primeval forest. Early sailors often anchored at "the Desert" to replenish their drinking water from the dark cypress pools found there. Cypress water tended to remain fresh for a long period of time, making it especially useful for sea voyages. English settlers, who landed at this spot in 1607, found fresh water springs, many varieties of trees, and dunes 100 feet tall.

Prior to 1770, fishermen often camped on the "the Desert." Several gentlemen, including Adam Keeling, who owned property to the west of the cape area, applied for patents on this stretch of land. In 1770, the fishermen protested to the governor and Council of State, claiming that such patents would be injurious to their livelihood. The petitioners were apparently successful in their request "that the Land remain a Common for Benefit of the Inhabitants of the Colony in General for Fisheries and other public uses."[2]

First Landing State Park

The Commonwealth owned "the Desert" until after the American Civil War. During the Reconstruction period, it was sold to lumber companies for the price of one dollar per acre. Due to the remoteness of the area, the lack of adequate transportation, and an extreme mosquito problem, lumbering operations were unsuccessful. In 1902, soon after the seaside resort community of Virginia Beach begin to develop, the Chesapeake Transit Company built a railroad to the beach by way of Cape Henry. Norfolk businessmen formed the Cape Henry Syndicate to buy and develop "the Desert."

The Commonwealth purchased the land from the syndicate and by 1936 had created Virginia Seashore State Park. Benjamin B. Burroughs was responsible for the formation of the Virginia Seashore State Park Association, and he became its first president. Six hundred workers from the Civilian Conservation Corps spent months building roads, trails, and cabins in order to make the natural beauty of the park accessible to visitors.

Seashore State Park opened to the general public on April 27, 1936. During World War II, the federal government purchased part of the park in order to add land to Fort Story.[3] In 1995, the name of the park was changed to First Landing State Park to better reflect the historical nature of the area.[4] On April 26, 1997 a ceremony was held at the park to re-inter the remains of sixty-four native Virginians from the Chesapeake tribe. The remains had been removed from the Great Neck area during construction in the 1970s and 1980s. The burial spot is near the visitor center and is enclosed by a split rail fence. The perimeter of the fence is encircled by dogwood trees.[5]

Today, First Landing State Park is still a beautiful area and is easily accessible to nature lovers. Because the park is located in an area of ecological transition, the variety of plant life is extremely large. The park includes the northernmost habitat of some types of flora, along with the southernmost occurrence of others. First Landing State Park is a haven for botanists and other students of wildlife, as well as those interested in geology. With dunes, sea, and inland waterways as its boundaries, the park area probably appears to visitors much the same as it did to the colonists when they landed at Cape Henry hundreds of years ago.[6]

Lighthouse

Fifty years after these first English settlers set foot on Cape Henry, the waters in the area were so congested that bonfires were used to guide vessels safely through the Chesapeake Bay. As early as 1727, the burgesses proposed that a lighthouse be built at Cape Henry, but taxes were high and interest waned. Twenty years later, the General Assembly passed an act for the erection and maintenance of a light at the cape. The funds were appropriated by a tonnage tax imposed on every ship that entered the Chesapeake Bay. A thirteen-man committee was appointed in 1752 to build a tower. This committee consisted of able, influential men of the time, but there is no evidence that they accomplished their task.

Another twenty years passed. In March 1773, the act was amended and £6,000 was appropriated to import stone for the lighthouse.[7] In September, the treasurer of the colony, Robert Carter Nicholas, ordered the materials and equipment from John Norton and Son, of London.[8] The April 28, 1774 edition of the *Virginia Gazette* in Williamsburg carried the following notice:

> *Notice is hereby given that a number of vessels will be wanted this summer to bring about 6,000 tons of stone from Mr. Brook's quarry on Rappahannock and land same on Cape Henry for the lighthouse, and the person or persons inclinable to engage in such work are desired to treat with Matthew Phripp, Paul Loyall and Thomas Newton, Esquire[9]*

After the Revolution, both the first United States Congress and the Assembly of Virginia enacted legislation specifically for the Cape Henry Lighthouse. The Commonwealth ceded a two-acre site on Cape Henry to the federal government, stipulating that the lighthouse be completed within seven years.[10] The $15,200 contract was signed in 1791 by Alexander Hamilton, U.S. Secretary of the Treasury, and John McComb, Jr., master architect.

The highest dune on Cape Henry was chosen for the construction site. At this spot, it was necessary to excavate twenty feet below the surface to find sand firm enough to support the foundation.[11] The Potomac sandstone, which had been quarried from Mr. Brooke's property sixteen years before, was used to build the lighthouse. The foundation was double-layered with rough stone bulwarks for protection again erosion.[12] At one point, work was delayed for many weeks when almost fifty tons of sand caved in on the excavation.[13]

The base of the lighthouse measures nearly thirty feet in diameter and is twenty feet below ground.[14] The octagonal tower rises to a height of seventy-two feet,[15] gradually sloping inward to a diameter of sixteen and one-half feet at the top. It is believed that the lighthouse was operating by October 1792, with Laban Gossigan as its first keeper. Oil lamps were used until 1812, when an Argand lamp with metallic reflectors was installed. A Jones fog bell was added in 1855, and a dioptric Fresnel lens, visible for twenty-four miles, was installed two years later.[16]

During the American Civil War, the Cape Henry Lighthouse was guarded by Union troops from Massachusetts who were later replaced by Black soldiers.[17] In April 1861, men from Princess Anne County attacked the lighthouse and destroyed its lamps and lens so that the United States government could not operate them. A Union lightship was moored in the bay until 1863, when the lighthouse was finally repaired.

In 1872, the district engineer reported that the lighthouse had become dangerously cracked and unsafe. Six years later, Congress appropriated $75,000 to construct a 150-foot tall cast-iron lighthouse with a concrete foundation.[18] The site chosen for the new tower was 357 feet from the old one.[19] Morris, Tasker & Company, of Philadelphia, assembled the iron work, and a brass and crystal lens was made in Paris.

Courtesy of the Old Coast Guard Station

Cape Henry Lighthouses
The original Cape Henry Lighthouse was in operation by October 1792. *right*
By 1872 the structure was considered unsafe. A cast-iron replacement, the tallest, fully-enclosed lighthouse in the United States, was completed in November 1881. *left*

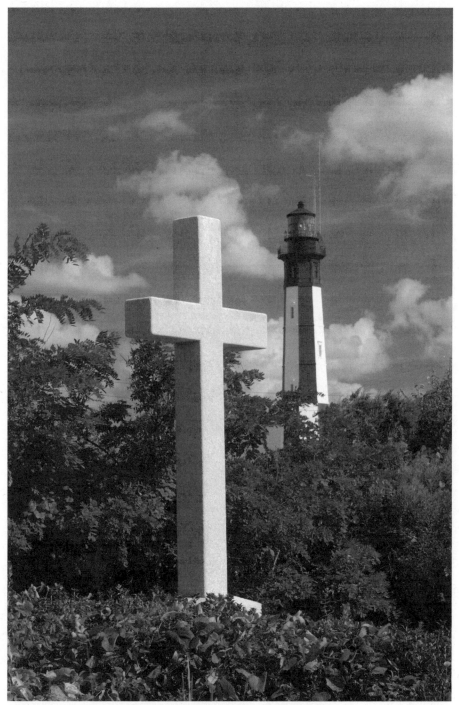

Courtesy of Carole J. Oste, Public Information Office, City of Virginia Beach

Cape Henry Lighthouse and Cape Henry Cross as seen today.

In order to land equipment and supplies at the construction site, a temporary pier was erected in August 1880. However, the first freight car to venture onto the pier plunged through its planks into the water, and the pier itself collapsed just three hours after the contractors had salvaged their supplies. An investigation revealed that marine borers had eaten through the pier's foundation. As a result of this mishap, a seven-mile railroad track was constructed to haul supplies by land from Lynnhaven Inlet to Cape Henry.

The second Cape Henry Lighthouse was completed in November 1881 as the tallest, fully-enclosed, cast-iron lighthouse in the United States. The new tower was fitted with a 160,000 candlepower[20] electric light in 1923. Cape Henry became the first radio-distance-finding station in the world in 1929, flashing the letter "U"[21] (designating an "unwatched" or automatic light without an attendant)[22] in Morse code at 80,000 candlepower.[23] In 1939, the U. S. Department of Commerce gave command of the newer lighthouse to the Fifth District of the United States Coast Guard.[24]

The original 1792 lighthouse was deeded to the Association for the Preservation of Virginia Antiquities (APVA) in 1930.[25] Today it is listed in the National Register of Historic Places and is open to sightseers.

Notes for Chapter 6

1. W. H. T. Squires, "Norfolk in By-Gone Days," *Norfolk Ledger Dispatch*, 4 February 1937, 6.
2. Katherine Fontaine Syer, "The County of Princess Anne, 1691 – 1957," in *The History of Lower Tidewater, Virginia*, vol. 2, ed. Rogers Dey Whichard (New York: Lewis Historical Publishing Company, Inc., 1959), 66-68.
3. Louisa Venable Kyle, "A Country Woman's Scrapbook: Seashore State Park – Its Natural Beauties Have Survived Since the Days of Exploration," *Norfolk Virginian-Pilot*, 16 May 1954, part 5, 3.
4. Guy Friddell, "Park's New Name Reflects Its History," *Virginian-Pilot and the Ledger-Star*, 3 May 1995, section B, 1.
5. Vandana Sinha, "Preserving the Past," *Virginian-Pilot*, 5 March 1999.
6. Syer, "The County of Princess Anne," 67-68.
7. Squires.
8. Katherine Fontaine Syer, "The Town and City of Virginia Beach," in *The History of Lower Tidewater, Virginia*, vol. 2, ed. Rogers Dey Whichard (New York: Lewis Historical Publishing Company, Inc., 1959), 124.
9. Squires.
10. Ibid.
11. Syer, "The Town and City of Virginia Beach," 124.
12. Squires.
13. Syer, "The Town and City of Virginia Beach," 124.
14. Ibid., 124-125.
15. Squires.
16. Syer, "The Town and City of Virginia Beach," 125.
17. "Gossip: Cape Henry Light Revisited by Keeper of Civil War Days," *The Tidewater Trail, Cape Henry Edition*, 1 July 1934, 3.
18. Syer, "The Town and City of Virginia Beach," 125-126.
19. Robert de Gast, *The Lighthouses of the Chesapeake* (Baltimore, Md.: The John Hopkins University Press, 1973), 13.
20. Syer, "The Town and City of Virginia Beach," 125-126.
21. de Gast, 13.
22. Gershom Bradford, *The Mariner's Dictionary* (Barre, Ma.: Barre Publishers, 1972), 286, 288.
23. de Gast, 13.
24. Syer, "The Town and City of Virginia Beach," 126.
25. de Gast, 13.

Chapter 7

Early Churches

Princess Anne County was created from the eastern section of Lower Norfolk County in 1691. An act of assembly in 1695 established that the existing boundaries of Lynnhaven Parish of the Anglican Church would be the boundaries of Princess Anne County as well. Lynnhaven Parish, in fact, was to serve as the county's only Anglican/Episcopal parish for two centuries, until 1895 when East Lynnhaven Parish was formed.

Early church services in Lynnhaven Parish were held in private homes. A May 15, 1637, entry in the Lower Norfolk County records ordered that a service be carried out at Captain Thorowgood's residence. A church building was in existence by the fall of 1639, and its first recorded vestry, or governing body, was chosen the following year. The church was erected on a site called Church Point, located on Adam Thorowgood's property. At his death, Thorowgood willed the church 1,000 pounds of tobacco with which to buy "some necessary and decent ornaments."[1]

Numerous Lower Norfolk County references indicated that this first church served the community until at least 1687. In 1691, the vestry contracted with Jacob Johnson for the construction of a brick church to replace the older structure, which had begun to deteriorate. The tidal waters of Lynnhaven Bay had gradually eroded Church Point to such an extent that the site of the old church building was undermined.

A new brick church, the second Lynnhaven Parish Church, was built on a two-acre site near the road to the ferry which crossed the Western Branch of the Lynnhaven River. This land was deeded to the vestry by Ebenezer Taylor. The construction contract specified that the church building be completed by the end of June 1692, or the builder would be fined 100,000 pounds of tobacco. The contractor was authorized to make use of the materials and furnishings from the abandoned Church Point structure. This second church served its parish for nearly forty years before it was outgrown.

By August 1733, the vestry had resolved to build a larger
church at Ferry Plantation, where the county already had a two-acre
site for a new courthouse. Three months later, however, the vestry
rescinded its previous resolution and unanimously agreed to build the

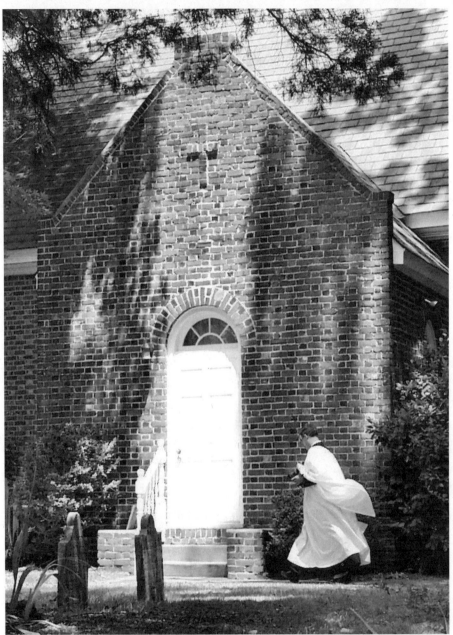

Courtesy of Carole J. Oste, Public Information Office, City of Virginia Beach

Old Donation Church, rebuilt circa 1916

new church adjacent to the old one. The new, larger church was probably built on the site of the 1695 frame courthouse, which was adjacent to the second church. The old church was converted into a public school.

Old Donation Episcopal Church, the third Lynnhaven Parish church, was accepted by the parish vestry on June 25, 1736. The first recorded reference to the name "Old Donation" appears in a vestry order dated 1822. According to tradition, the name originated in 1776 when The Reverend Robert Dickson willed land adjoining the Lynnhaven church site to the parish. The bequest was to be used to endow a free school. There is little doubt that the present Old Donation Episcopal Church building is the third Lynnhaven Parish church, parts of which date back to 1736.[2]

With the end of the American Revolution came the demise of the Church of England in America. During the Revolution some ministers had remained loyal to England, while others had fought against the British. As it owed allegiance to the crown, the Anglican Church was disestablished in the colonies.[3] Church property was left to deteriorate until the Protestant Episcopal Church of Virginia was established in 1785. The Episcopal Church grew slowly as the ranks of clergy were depleted and the bishops who could ordain priests were English. American bishops needed to be consecrated for the new denomination.

It was not until 1842 that The Reverend John G. Hull instituted a reorganization of the parish. Emmanuel Episcopal Church was built at Kempsville and Old Donation Episcopal Church was abandoned for regular worship.

For forty years, Old Donation remained substantially unused, and in 1882 it was completely gutted by a forest fire. To keep the church site from reverting to the Commonwealth, a religious service had to be conducted there at least once a year. Thurmer Hoggard IV and a few other stalwart parishioners made annual pilgrimages to the burned-out church to hold services. The congregation of Emmanuel Episcopal Church collected funds for Old Donation's restoration. In 1916 the parishioners' dedication was rewarded when Old Donation was rebuilt.[5] It would not regain its former status as the "parent church" of Lynnhaven Parish until October 12, 1943, when Emmanuel Episcopal Church was destroyed by fire.[6] Old Donation Episcopal Church is located at 4449 North Witchduck Road.

Among Old Donation's prized possessions are its colonial silver communion pieces. The paten was acquired in 1711 as a gift from Maximilian Boush and is engraved with his coat of arms. The chalice (dated 1712) and the flagon (dated 1716) were given to the church from Queen Anne's Bounty. (Two years after Princess Anne became queen, she set aside for the "use of the Established Church in its poor livings, sixteen thousand pounds a year under the name of 'Queen Anne's Bounty.'")[7] The marble font and pewter alms basin are said to have come from the original Lynnhaven Parish Church at Church Point.[8]

The county was also served by several smaller Anglican churches known as "chapels of ease." Since the parish boundaries were so extensive, it was often a hardship for isolated settlers to attend the principal parish church, thus services were held at various outlying chapels. There are early references to the Eastern Branch Chapel and the Southern Shore Parish Church, both located on the Eastern Branch of the Elizabeth River.

The Eastern Shore Chapel (or "lower chapel") has offered nearly continuous service since before 1689. A court order of

Courtesy of the Eastern Shore Chapel

The Communion Silver of the Eastern Shore Chapel
The flagon, paten-cover, and chalice were made in London, circa 1759-1760, with maker's mark "WG" for William Grundy.

September 1689 called for the construction for a frame courthouse on Edward Cooper's land near a chapel of ease on the eastern shore of the Lynnhaven River. This chapel of ease, the first Eastern Shore Chapel, stood at the southern end of Great Neck at the north fork of Wolfsnare Creek. The log structure was replaced by a larger frame chapel built in November 1726 on Joel Cornick's Salisbury Plains plantation.

In October 1753, the vestry resolved to replace the frame chapel with an even larger brick structure modeled after the parent church, Old Donation.[9] This 1754 chapel served the community until the American Civil War, when it was used as an army stable. Even though the sky blue interior was badly damaged, services were held there again in 1866.[10]

Due to expansion of the Naval Air Station at Oceana in the early 1950s, the third Eastern Shore Chapel was razed.[11] On March 12, 1954, the fourth and present chapel was completed on a nine-acre tract on Laskin Road, with an additional eleven-acre cemetery. The pews, stained glass windows, and baptismal font were salvaged from the old chapel.[12] Like Old Donation, Eastern Shore Chapel has colonial silver communion pieces that date back to 1759. According to local belief, these communion pieces were buried in a henhouse for safekeeping because of the Union occupation during the Civil War.[13]

The Eastern Shore Chapel had as its mission the Chapel by the Sea at Dam Neck. This chapel was unique in that it was built with lumber from the three-master barque *Agnes Barton*, wrecked in 1889 near the Dam Neck Mills Lifesaving Station. The Chapel by the Sea served its congregation until 1924, when it was bought by Christ Church of Norfolk and remodeled into a recreation camp for girls.[14]

The southern interior of the county was served by Pungo Chapel. (Pungo is a shortened version of the Indian name "Machipongo," which was also the name of the region.)[15] The first of three Pungo Chapel buildings may have been situated at the lower end of Pungo Ridge, on the peninsula between the present North Landing River and Back Bay. It was erected in this remote area as a result of a 200-acre endowment given by Captain Hugh Campbell in 1692. This endowment was for the support of lay readers in the remote parish areas of Somerton (Nansemond County), Blackwater (Isle of Wight), and North River (Princess Anne County).[16]

Pungo Chapel, the first "upper chapel" of the parish, was a frame building with no brick foundation. In March 1739, James James was contracted to replace it with a brick structure. The new site was located on William Dyer's land, which made it less remote than the first chapel. Dyer served as sexton and was reimbursed for keeping the chapel clean and for digging a well.

By June 1772, the second Pungo Chapel was in a dangerous state of disrepair and another, even larger, brick chapel was built in 1773. This chapel, built by Hardress Waller, was probably the largest church building in the Lynnhaven Parish. This last Pungo Chapel was built in the vicinity of the second chapel on a one-acre plot of land belonging to Anthony Fentress. According to George Carrington Mason, the third Pungo Chapel was probably built on the east side of Pungo Ridge Road, directly opposite the home of W. G. Eaton. This chapel declined through the years and eventually fell into ruin. The Clerk of the Pungo Chapel periodically conducted services at reading places established in extremely remote areas where no chapels existed, such as Blackwater and Knott's Island.[17]

Colonial records indicate that religious dissenters also worshipped in Princess Anne County. Quakers, or the Society of Friends, were considered the "extreme left" of the English Reformation and were harassed and persecuted by local county officials.[18] William Berkeley, the royal governor of Virginia, admonished prominent county gentlemen "to have an Exact care of this Pestilent sect of ye Quakers."[19] In 1662 and 1663, over twenty people were fined for attending Quaker meetings. Richard Russell was fined for holding meetings in his house.[20]

The Quakers eventually migrated to Nansemond County and did not return to Princess Anne County for nearly three centuries. In 1954, Mr. and Mrs. Robert D. Wilson, finding no Quaker Meeting House in the area, decided to have meetings in their home. Later, with the help of fellow Quakers from North Carolina, their group built a meeting house and a school on Laskin Road.

A group of Presbyterian dissenters had a meeting house on Edward Cooper's plantation at Great Neck, near the first Eastern Shore Chapel. The meeting house was a registered place of worship by 1693. Services were conducted by The Reverend Josias Mackie, who had previously been dismissed from the Elizabeth River Parish for being a radical nonconformist. By 1699, The Reverend Mackie was conducting additional services at a private home in his former Elizabeth River Parish.

Baptist dissenters in Princess Anne County had their first meeting house in Pungo. John Whitehead deeded half an acre of land with an existing structure to the Baptists in July 1764. The original building was eventually replaced and named Oak Grove Baptist Church in 1856. In 1774, an offshoot of this Pungo congregation established the Blackwater Baptist Church, situated north of the Blackwater River. This church received its first permanent minister in 1803.

Following the American Revolution, the Baptist movement experienced a great revival. Eastern Shore Baptist Church was established in 1784 as a result of this tremendous growth. Its name was later changed to London Bridge Baptist Church. The original church building burned in 1946, but the congregation continues today with modern facilities. In 1835, the London Bridge congregation established a mission at Princess Anne Courthouse, which became known as St. John's Baptist Church in 1856. Kempsville Baptist Church is another old church in Princess Anne County, having been established in 1814.

Charity Methodist Church was built at Back Bay in 1789 and was the first of its denomination in Princess Anne County. It was followed in 1791 by Old Nimmo Church, a picturesque county landmark famous for its camp meetings. Francis Asbury, the first American Methodist bishop, preached there soon after it was built.[21]

In 1872, several members of Old Nimmo who were former slaves, broke away from the church in order to meet in private homes. By 1873, the congregation had moved into a tiny log cabin located near Old Nimmo. The cabin was situated on an acre of land which had been purchased by the congregation from Durant Simmons for one dollar. The deed was recorded under the name of Mount Zion African Methodist Episcopal Church. A few years later, the congregation built a log church, and in 1907 the present Mount Zion was completed.[22] Mount Zion A.M.E. Church is located at 2268 Princess Anne Road.

St. Mark A.M.E. Church, located at 1740 Potters Road, was also established after the end of the Civil War. The earliest worship services were held in a log cabin on land given to the congregation by E. D. Ferebee, a local resident. The original cabin burned and was replaced by a frame building in the late 1800s. During the early 1940s, the second structure was torn down and the current church building was completed.[23]

Another quaint church was the Wash Woods Methodist Church, which served the coastal settlements at Little Island, False Cape, Sandbridge, and Wash Woods. This church was built out of cypress lumber salvaged from the cargo of the wrecked three-master schooner *John S. Woods*, which ran aground in 1895 during a severe winter storm. The church had no regular minister. Circuit riders served the congregation until the building was abandoned in 1922.[24]

During the twentieth century, the population of the area now known as Virginia Beach increased greatly and, as a result, has become significantly more diverse. Today, Virginia Beach is home to a multitude of churches and religious organizations representing a wide variety of denominations and beliefs.

Notes for Chapter 7

1. George Carrington Mason, *Colonial Churches of Tidewater, Virginia* (Richmond, Va.: Whittet and Shepperson, 1945), 129-130.
2. Ibid., 133-139.
3. Floyd McKnight, "The Town and City of Suffolk," in *The History of Lower Tidewater, Virginia,* vol. 2, ed. Rogers Dey Whichard (New York: Lewis Historical Publishing Company, Inc., 1959), 168.
4. Mason, 147-148.
5. Katherine Fontaine Syer, "The County of Princess Anne, 1691-1957," in *The History of Lower Tidewater, Virginia,* vol. 2, ed. Rogers Dey Whichard (New York: Lewis Historical Publishing Company, Inc., 1959), 89.
6. Mason, 148.
7. Syer, 88.
8. Mason, 148.
9. Ibid., 141-144.
10. Ibid., 148.
11. Syer, 90.
12. Louisa Venable Kyle, "A Country Woman's Scrapbook: Fourth Eastern Shore Chapel Almost Ready for Its Congregation and Their Services," *Norfolk Virginian-Pilot,* 14 March 1954, part 5, 4.
13. Mason, 148.
14. Louisa Venable Kyle, " A Country Woman's Scrapbook Tossed Up by Stormy Seas, Ships That Became
Chapels – Abandoned Now – These Fall Prey to Time and Decay," *Norfolk Virginian-Pilot,* 9 November 1952, part 2,8.
15. Mason, 145.
16. Ibid., 149-150.
17. Ibid., 145-147.
18. Syer, 93.
19. Edward Wilson James, ed., *The Lower Norfolk County Virginia Antiquary,* vol. IV (New York: P. Smith, 1951), 78.
20. Ibid., 78-79.
21. Syer, 93-95.
22. Mary Reid Barrow, "The History Beat: Civil War Marked Beginning of Black Churches," *The Beacon,* 8-9 July 1982, 6.
23. Margie Hurlbut, "Old Church: Fresh Ideas," *Virginia Beach Beacon,* 28 May 1972, 2.
24. Kyle, "Tossed Up by Stormy Seas."

Chapter 8

Courthouses

The churches and the courts were the hub of the colonial community's existence. Because the Anglican Church was the established church – that is, legally and financially tied to the government – many of its functions were civic ones. These included oversight of morals, levying of taxes, care of the poor, and certification of land boundaries. When the Anglican Church was disestablished in 1784, these activities, formerly provided by church vestries, devolved on county officials.[1] Until that time the churches and the courts worked in tandem.

The early courts met in the Lynnhaven area, probably on land owned by Adam Thorowgood. In 1689, Lower Norfolk County commissioners ordered a courthouse built on the north fork of Wolfsnare Creek near the first Eastern Shore Chapel. The location at the Eastern Shore Settlement, then a thriving community, became the county seat when Princess Anne was established in 1691.[2]

In 1695, the county commissioners ordered construction of a new courthouse "upon land belonging to the Brick Church." The courthouse at the chapel was disassembled and shipped across to the west side of the Lynnhaven River. The materials were used to construct the slightly larger 1695 frame courthouse.[3] The building was to be thirty-five feet long and twenty feet wide and divided into a room for the court and a jury room. The jail was to be provided with "good posts sett so close that nor man can get through and jousts also so close and neare together and that there be stocks and pillory sett up by the court house."[4]

The next courthouse was located at the ferry which crossed the Lynnhaven River, also on the west side. This tract of land was known as "the Ferry." In 1730, Charles Smyth deeded the county two acres at the ferry for a new court building. It was to be the first courthouse in Princess Anne County to be built of brick. This site became known as Ferry Farm or Old Donation Farm and is located off Pembroke Boulevard. It has been suggested that the iron bars on the existing

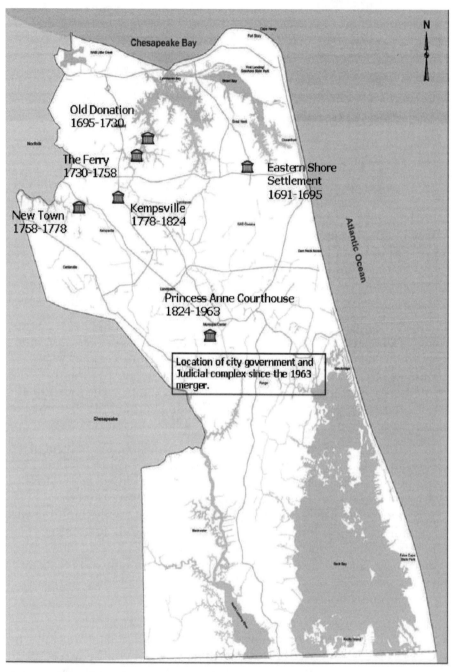

Courtesy of City of Virginia Beach, ComIT, GIS Mapping

Virginia Beach Courthouses

Ferry Farm house indicate that this was the room in which Grace Sherwood was held when she was jailed. However, that is unlikely, as the deed of the two acres for the courthouse postdates her trial.[5]

The courthouse was moved to New Town in 1758. The village, established in 1697 on the north side of the Eastern Branch of the Elizabeth River, was a vibrant colonial settlement because both the Eastern Branch of the Elizabeth River and Broad Creek were navigable. New Town was a port of entry and had a customhouse and a British garrison. The Walkes, the Moseleys, and other influential families lived in the area. The church and court association continued as the town site adjoined the Lynnhaven Parish Eastern Branch Chapel.[6]

In 1778, the court moved to Kempe's Landing, which was incorporated as the town of Kempsville in 1783. Until suitable structures could be built, the court met temporarily at George Logan's dry goods store, and his wet goods store was converted into the jail.[7] A brick courthouse and a frame jail were built. The jail burned down and was replaced in 1780 with an English bond brick structure, located behind the Peter Singleton house known as Pleasant Hall. When the county seat moved again, the courthouse was converted into a Baptist church. The jail became Kempsville Academy, a private school, and later a private residence.[8] The courthouse was demolished in 1971 after attempts to renovate it failed.[9] The jail was in poor condition for many years and was bulldozed in 1974.[10]

The county court remained at Kempsville until 1824, when it was moved to a location at the geographic center of the county. The area was then known as "The Cross Roads" and is now known as the Virginia Beach Municipal Center. The commissioners entered into a contract to build the courthouse, clerk's office, and jail. The contract specifically noted the types of brick, thickness of walls, and kinds of wood to be used. The contract was executed in 1820, with a completion date of 1822. However, the court did not move from Kempsville until 1824.[11]

The Princess Anne Courthouse was subjected to so many renovations and additions that it was denied Virginia State Historical Landmark Status in 1981. Much of the interior was deemed historically compromised and virtually only the outside bricks remained of the original 1824 building. While denying the application, a state architectural historian noted that the "decision does not mean that the building is not of historical significance to the City of Virginia Beach."[12] An adjacent two-story jail building,

Courtesy of the Sargeant Memorial Room, Norfolk Public Libraries

Princess Anne Courthouse was built in 1824 and was used until the opening of the Judicial Center in 1993. It is currently used as office space.

Courtesy of Carole J. Oste, Public Information Office, City of Virginia Beach

Judicial Center, which opened in 1993 is the venue for court and legal administrative functions.

which also housed the jailer and his family, was abandoned in 1947. It was reputed to be the site of an 1898 hanging, which was the last to take place in Princess Anne County. A chimney collapsed in March 1964, ending a debate on the feasibility of saving the building. The jail was demolished soon thereafter.[13]

By the 1980s, it had become clear that the 1824 courthouse and its additions were not adequate for the growing city of Virginia Beach. In 1993, a 317,000-square-foot Judicial Center was dedicated. The complex includes space for thirty-two courtrooms, court processing and administrative functions, a law library, and an underground passage from the jail to the courts building.[14]

Notes for Chapter 8

1. Charles Francis Cocke, *Parish Lines Diocese of Virginia* (Richmond, Va.: The Virginia State Library, 1967), 10-11.

2. Katherine Fontaine Syer, "The County of Princess Anne, 1691-1957" in *The History of Lower Tidewater, Virginia*, vol. 2, ed. Rogers Dey Whichard (New York: Lewis Historical Publishing Company, Inc., 1959), 55.

3. Syer, 60.

4. *Princess Anne Order Book*, 1691-1709, part I, handwritten copy, n.d., of entry dated 12 September 1695, 87.

5. Sadie Scott Kellam and V. Hope Kellam, *Old Houses in Princess Anne Virginia* (Portsmouth, Va.: Printcraft, 1931), 189-190.

6. Syer, 69.

7. Edward Wilson James, ed., *The Lower Norfolk County Antiquary*, vol. II, (New York: P. Smith, 1951), 133.

8. Glenn Kittler, "State Landmark at Kempsville Listed for Sale," *Norfolk Virginian-Pilot*, 26 September 1948, part 3, 18.

9. Jack Dorsey, "Old Kempsville Courthouse Falls to Bulldozer's Work," *Virginia Beach Beacon*, 18 November 1971, 1.

10. Helen Crist, "Landmark Flattened by Bulldozer," *Virginia Beach Beacon*, 11 July 1974, 1.

11. Mary Reid Barrow, "Old Courthouse Set the Style: Nothing But the Best," *Virginia Beach Beacon*, 10 September 1981, 6.

12. Marc Davis, "Courthouse Is Rejected as Landmark," *Virginian-Pilot*, 30 December 1981, section D, 1.

13. Chet Paschang, "Fallen Chimney May Lead to Demolition of P.A. Jail," *Ledger-Star*, 17 March 1964, 25.

14. Marc Davis, "Beach Brings Order to Its Courts with New, Bigger, Safer Center," *Virginian-Pilot*, 10 September 1981, *Beacon*, 6.

Chapter 9

War on Princess Anne Soil

The Revolutionary War

Thehe American Revolution brought civil strife to the people of Princess Anne County. Many citizens were loyal to the Commonwealth and opposed British oppression. These citizens offered their fortunes and their lives to advance the cause of independence.

The Earl of Dunmore, the last royal governor of Virginia, was in command of British forces in the Commonwealth. Early in 1775, Lord Dunmore grew anxious due to the deterioration of his power and position. On April 20, 1775, the day after the Battle of Lexington and Concord,[1] he authorized the removal of gunpowder stored in the magazine at Williamsburg. The citizens were outraged and the flames of rebellion were kindled.[2] Lord Dunmore dissolved the House of Burgesses. In response the Burgesses moved to Raleigh Tavern and thus Virginia's revolutionary government, the Virginia Convention, was formed.[3]

In an effort to reassert his authority, Lord Dunmore dispatched British troops to Kempsville (then known as Kempe's Landing) on October 15, 1775. Soldiers pillaged the area and destroyed the firearms stored there.[4] The local militia, known as "Shirtmen" because of their buckskin hunting shirts, engaged the British troops in combat.[5] Thomas Mathews, captain of this Virginia militia unit, was captured. He was the first patriot prisoner of war taken on Virginia soil.

On November 7, 1775, Dunmore proclaimed martial law, declaring all persons bearing arms against the British Crown to be traitors.[6] He also offered freedom to all slaves who would join His Majesty's segregated "Ethiopian Regiment."[7]

Lord Dunmore's forces were returning to Norfolk from Great Bridge on November 16, 1775. This was an attempt to fortify Norfolk for the royal government.[8] The Virginia Convention was determined that Lord Dunmore should not hold Norfolk and ordered Virginia troops to go there and drive him out.[9] The local militia of Princess Anne and Norfolk counties assembled at Kempsville. The patriots, aware of Lord Dunmore's approach, set their troops in ambush formation. Dunmore walked into the trap.

What could have been a patriot victory, however, turned into an embarrassing disappointment. The ill-disciplined local militia fortified their courage with drink while lying in wait for the British troops. When the troops marched up, the "Shirtmen" did not attack or open fire. Instead, they fled to the woods, some soldiers being too drunk even to run away.[10] John Ackiss, a local "Shirtman," was killed on the field. He was the first Virginia soldier to lose his life in the battle for independence. Colonel Anthony Lawson and Colonel Joseph Hutchings, along with eight others, were wounded and taken prisoner.[11] Colonels Lawson and Hutchings were released the following year in exchange for British loyalist officers Jacob Ellegood and Alexander Gordon.[12] (A stone monument at the corner of Overland Road and Princess Anne Road commemorates "The Skirmish of Kempsville.")

The colonists were incensed by Dunmore's many hostile actions, his infringement on their rights and liberties, and his seizure of their property. An ordinance was enacted by the Virginia Convention on December 1, 1775, which increased military force by directing six additional patriot regiments to be raised.[13]

The British retaliated by burning Norfolk on New Year's Day, 1776. Colonel Robert Howe removed his patriot forces from Norfolk the following month and garrisoned them at Kempsville, Great Bridge, and Suffolk. Historian William H. Stewart writes that Norfolk residents were forced "to seek shelter from the rigors of winter. The good people of Suffolk received these distressed refugees with open doors and unbounded hospitality until every building in the town was crowded."[14]

The Virginia Committee of Safety was charged with the duty of deciding the number of minutemen to be drafted in each county or borough.[15] The committee appointed the following men to serve as deputies for Princess Anne County: William Robinson, Thomas Reynolds Walker, Thomas Old, John Thoroughgood, James Henley, Erasmus Haynes, and William Wishart. These deputies were also responsible for identifying loyalist sympathizers. With a quorum of four or more deputies, a May 1776 entry in the *Calendar of Virginia State Papers* states that these men "having taken an oath before a magistrate . . . to do equal and impartial justice and to keep each other's secrets, do assemble themselves together and make strict inquiry into the temper and former conduct of the inhabitants . . . of Princess Anne . . . ." The deputies were to ascertain who supported the cause of independence, who was neutral, and who was a sympathizer to the British crown.[16]

Indifference to the patriot cause should not be confused with loyalty to the British Crown.[17] To continue conducting business, Loyalist merchants had to take the oath of allegiance and wear a badge of red cloth on their chests.[18]

Several local merchants were avowed loyalists. George Logan, one such merchant who chose to return to Scotland,[19] was tried in absentia on charges of treason in 1778. Logan was found guilty, and his dry goods storehouse at Kempe's Landing was appropriated for use as a courthouse.[20] John Saunders also was declared a British subject. He returned to England where he became an officer in the British Army.[21] Saunders's brother-in-law, Colonel Jacob Ellegood, was forced to leave his Rose Hall plantation. He sought security by setting up residence in New Brunswick, Canada.[22]

During the five years prior to Cornwallis's surrender at Yorktown, Norfolk and Princess Anne counties gave every indication of having a nest of loyalists. Colonel Thomas Newton, Jr. wrote to Governor Thomas Nelson that Princess Anne was

> *the enemy's country with many loyalists living in affluence, and having plenty of specie at their command, claiming the privilege of paroles, whilst the good men who left their homes are starving for want of necessaries, having no hard money to buy with and others do everything in their power to prevent the paper from passing.*[23]

Colonel William Wishart, with the assistance of Colonel Dabney, initiated a campaign of vengeance against the loyalist sympathizers in Princess Anne County.[24] The following persons were confined for treason for bearing arms against their county: Samuel Craft, Thomas Grimstead, Ethered Grimstead, Southern Cartwrite, William Hutchins, Elias Davis, Tecle Clay, and John Cooper. Rolly Grimstead was jailed for bearing arms against his county and forcing others into service. John Brown and James Weaver were also incarcerated for treasonable practices.[25] At the special local court called to try the traitors, three men could not be found to act as judges, and a near riot ensued. Although there was "sufficient proof to hang many of them if the Court was to sit here [in Norfolk]; but the witnesses have not money to bear their expenses to Richmond, & the most atrocious villains will escape. . . ."[26]

The Battle Off The Virginia Capes

The little known Battle of the Capes, fought off Cape Charles and Cape Henry, was a major naval engagement between the French and British, marking the turning point of the American Revolution.

General Washington's ultimate plan was to surround the British so they were trapped and could not retreat. On the land in Yorktown, he had them exactly where he wanted them and victory was probable if the British Navy could be kept away. The British knew that they could succeed in rescuing Cornwallis and his men as long as their ships ultimately could return to a seaport. With the Americans having so few ships, the British Navy could go where it pleased and move soldiers faster than General Washington. The Americans needed a naval presence, and the French filled that void.

France wanted to help the Americans. Thirty years earlier, the British had captured France's Canadian colonies, and the French feared a similar attack would be mounted to overtake the French colonies in the West Indies. Both France and Great Britain kept fleets on patrol in the West Indies, and Admiral de Grasse had commanded the French fleet there.

Even though he was a nobleman, the young Comte de Grasse went to sea at the age of 12 and had participated in many sea battles in his 50 years in the French Navy. Unlike many officers who were awarded their jobs because of important family ties, Admiral de Grasse was a seasoned fighter and knew how to win battles. When he received letters in July 1781 asking for ships, soldiers, and money to help General Washington and the American cause, he acted promptly. He gathered the ships in his West Indies fleet, paid for the transport of French Army soldiers, convinced the Spanish in Cuba to aide the cause, and headed north.

Meanwhile Admiral Rodney, commander of the British West Indies Fleet, chose to send only a portion of his ships to aid his countrymen fighting in America. His small fleet made a cursory check of the Chesapeake Bay, saw no French ships, and wrongly assumed that Admiral de Grasse had sailed back to the West Indies. Admiral Rodney then directed his fleet to New York to join the British Army. He guessed incorrectly that New York would be the scene of General Washington's next attack.

General Washington was busy hurrying his troops to Yorktown as Admiral de Grasse's fleet was headed to the Chesapeake Bay. The French fleet arrived five days after the British had passed the Virginia capes. De Grasse sent some of his ships to move General Washington's army, and then anchored. He awaited a small supplemental French fleet due from Rhode Island carrying much needed supplies. A major concern for de Grasse was keeping the British Navy from intercepting this second French fleet as well as keeping them out of the Chesapeake Bay.

Finally, the British ships from the West Indies arrived in New York bearing Admiral Rodney's message that the French vessels had

Courtesy of the U.S. Naval Academy Museum

Admiral de Grasse
French Admiral de Grasse and his fleet were instrumental in helping American forces win The Battle Off the Virginia Capes.

disappeared from the region. When the combined British fleet left
New York for the Chesapeake Bay, British Admiral Graves had no idea
that the entire French West Indies Fleet was waiting for him in
Virginia.

Upon their arrival, Admiral de Grasse sailed out into the
Atlantic to meet the British Navy, giving General Washington time to
advance to Yorktown. He also was keeping the British occupied so
they would not capture the French fleet from Rhode Island.

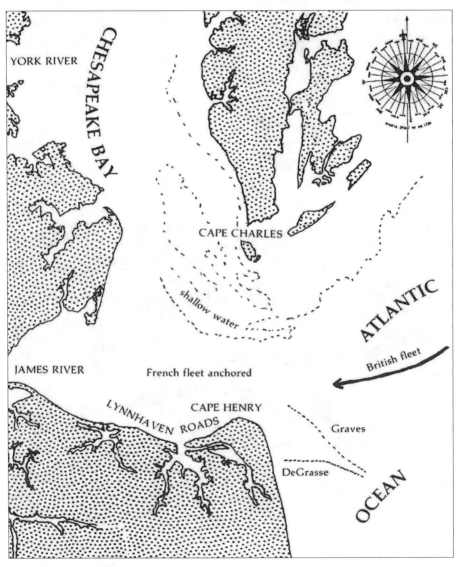

Battle of the Virginia Capes

On September 5, 1781, the French Admiral locked horns with the most powerful Navy in the world, and England lost its American colonies. Lord Cornwallis and 8,000 British soldiers sat in the Chesapeake Bay, awaiting assistance from British Naval forces. Unfortunately for the British, French ships arrived first, effectively cutting off the British Navy from their rescuers. For any hope of success, Admiral Graves had to align his ships, take advantage of a tail wind, and chase off the French Navy. The French contingent of ships outnumbered the British 24 to 19, but the British were ready for the fight.

Led by Admiral de Grasse, the French fleet had been anchored next to the Lynnhaven Bay, and many of the men were ashore. The French ships readied to leave minus many crew members, then sailed against the wind and tide toward Cape Henry. They spread apart once they were on the open ocean. This made the French fleet easy opponents for the British Navy, and the battle could have been a British victory. However, the British refused to stray from their accepted tenets of naval warfare. Fearing court-martial, Admiral Graves unwaveringly followed the *Fighting Instructions*, a set of required rules by which all British naval officers commanded. Thus, the British missed an opportunity that could have changed the outcome of the Revolutionary War.

Fighting Instructions decreed that the best way to win a sea battle was to line up next to the enemy's ships and fire cannon shots until the ships sank. Admiral Graves directed the vessels of the British fleet to line up parallel to the enemy. The proper alignment could not be obtained. The ships in front were close enough to engage in battle, but the ships in the rear were too far away and could not assist in the bombardment. Repositioning of the ships could have made a huge difference in the outcome of the battle. Unless the Admiral sent a flagged signal for the ships to change position, however, no British vessel would ever break alignment. That signal never came. The ships in the rear stayed put and never fought.

Another British error soon became apparent. The British tried to sink enemy ships by punching holes in them with cannon fire. The French were much better shots and aimed for the masts and sails of the British vessels. Without sails, the British ships were helpless.

When the sun set that day in early September 1781, the fighting ceased. Several British ships were so damaged they could no longer fight, and one never made it back to the home port. British casualties numbered 336 dead or wounded, while the French lost 221 sailors. More sailors died in this battle than soldiers did in the Battle of Yorktown. Aboard their flagship, the *Ville de Paris*, victory looked elusive to the French. Although Admiral de Grasse failed to capture or to sink any enemy ships, he succeeded in his charge from General Washington and assured that Lord Cornwallis was not rescued.

At the conclusion of the battle, the British and French fleets watched each other over the course of the next five days. Then de Grasse sailed back into the Chesapeake Bay where he found his French compatriots waiting, for they had circled far around the battle zone and slipped unnoticed into the Bay.

It was impossible for Admiral Graves to get his damaged vessels past Admiral de Grasse's ships and the French reinforcements from Rhode Island. He retreated to New York for a month to patch up his battered fleet. He started out again on October 19, attempting to rescue the still stranded Cornwallis. The attempt was too late, however, as this was the very day Cornwallis finally gave up waiting for rescue and surrendered to General Washington.

When Washington captured Yorktown, he was well aware that the Battle off the Virginia Capes had provided him the opportunity to win the war. In a letter to de Grasse, Washington thanked the French Admiral, "In the name of America, for the glorious event for which she is indebted to you." De Grasse's reply was simple yet eloquent: "I consider myself infinitely happy to have been of some service to the United States.[27]"

The War of 1812

While Princess Anne County suffered civil strife during the Revolution, it escaped with only slight damage during the War of 1812. This war actually began in the waters off Princess Anne County. The United States frigate *Chesapeake* was ordered to the Mediterranean. The ship sailed from Norfolk on June 22, 1807, to relieve the USS *Constitution*. The *Chesapeake* was still undergoing repairs. Her cannons were unmounted and her crew was inexperienced. The HBMS *Leopard,* fully aware of the *Chesapeake*'s helpless condition, awaited her off Lynnhaven Inlet and followed in her wake until the *Chesapeake* halted. The British demanded the immediate surrender of four *Chesapeake* crew members. When the Americans refused to surrender, the British opened fire at close range, killing three men and wounding eighteen. The British seized four sailors, and the crippled *Chesapeake* returned to Norfolk.

While the country was extremely indignant about this treatment, the diplomacy of Presidents Thomas Jefferson and James

Madison postponed open hostilities for almost five years. President Madison's war manifesto dated June 19, 1812, listed British violations of the American flag on the high seas, impressment of American seamen, and harassment of American vessels in their own harbors as causes for the war.[28]

After war was declared, it was assumed that the British navy would attack or blockade the ports and harbors of the Chesapeake Bay. General Robert Taylor, a Norfolk lawyer, was given command of the Chesapeake Bay's defenses and instituted a series of shore watchposts from Cape Henry to Norfolk. The British made amphibious landings near Chesapeake Beach, where they burned the watchpost and attempted a landing south of Cape Henry.[29] The county militia repelled them each time.

During the Cape Henry assault, a British frigate bombarded the coast near the area now known as Seatack.[30] Admiral Sir George Warren's fleet anchored in Lynnhaven Bay, and all ports and harbors of the Chesapeake Bay were declared blockaded on February 5, 1812. The British continued to exert their naval supremacy until the end of the hostilities.[31]

The American Civil War

During the conflicts of the Civil War, Princess Anne County was spared most of the bloody ravages experienced by other Virginia counties. The 20th Virginia Regiment was composed of six to eight companies of the local militia.[32] Two companies of the 15th Virginia Cavalry were also comprised of local soldiers. Company "B" was formed from the Chesapeake Light Cavalry of Lynnhaven Beach, and Company "C" was composed of the Princess Anne Cavalry.[33]

The Seaboard Rifles were organized as a state militia unit at London Bridge in December 1859. When the 6th Virginia Infantry was formed in Norfolk, the Seaboard Rifles were incorporated into it as Company "F." Company "B" of the 6th Virginia Infantry was comprised of the Princess Anne Grays.[34] The 6th Virginia Infantry saw action at numerous major battles of the war, such as Malvern Hill, the Seven Days Battles, Antietam, Chancellorsville, Gettysburg, the Petersburg Siege, and Appomattox Court House.[35]

With the advent of hostilities in 1861, two skirmishes occurred in Princess Anne County. The first occurred in April when the local militia attacked the Cape Henry Lighthouse and destroyed the lens.[36] The second skirmish occurred on October 19 when a Confederate battery at Lynnhaven Bay fired on the USS *Daylight* in the Chesapeake Bay.[37] In 1861, while General Robert E. Lee was at Rolleston in Princess Anne County, the plans for an supposedly invulnerable floating ironclad battery were formed. These plans would convert the CSS *Merrimac* into the CSS *Virginia*.[38]

Norfolk and the surrounding area was later evacuated by the Confederate forces. On May 10, 1862, Federal troops moved in and established a military district under the command of Brigadier General Egbert L. Viele (1862-March 1863) and later Brigadier General Benjamin F. Butler (March 1863-1864). In effect, Norfolk and Princess Anne counties were detached from the rest of Virginia. Martial law was imposed, personal property was seized, and the economy deteriorated. Recognized by the Federals, the "restored government of Francis Pierpont at Alexandria City"[39] enforced restrictions on the populace. Physicians were not permitted to practice unless they swore allegiance to the federal government. Creditors and landlords were not permitted to collect debts or repossess their property unless they had first taken the oath of allegiance to the Union.[40]

Federal forces were garrisoned at key positions around Princess Anne County. Federal troops pursued guerilla bands, blockade runners, and smugglers pillaging the county. While the local citizens offered passive resistance to the Union forces, roving Confederate guerilla bands incessantly harassed the Federal troops. The guerilla warfare became so effective that Federal patrols were ordered to force half a dozen of the most influential local secessionists to act as guides to find the guerillas.[41]

Destruction of the county's bridges was a prime guerilla activity. In retaliation, the Federal forces issued special orders requiring that prominent secessionists in the immediate vicinity keep the bridges repaired. Bartlett Smith, Dr. Tibault, Mr. Forbes, Thomas Keeling, J. P. Keeling, John Duffey, Horatio Cornick, Henry Gornto, Martin Harris, Charles Brooks, and Swepson Brooks were ordered to rebuild the bridge at London Bridge within ten days, or they would be imprisoned and their personal property sold to repair it.[42]

The guerillas had their headquarters at Fog Island. In September 1863 a force of 130 Federal troops marched on Fog Island, but the guerillas escaped through the swamps towards Knott's Island. On September 23, while scouting Back Bay, the Federal infantry discovered a rendezvous of blockade runners. Three boats were destroyed and eleven people were captured.[43] On September 30 the Back Bay saltworks belonging to "Denis Huel, . . . B. Carson, . . . and a Mr. Sandis" were destroyed by Captain Kerr's Federal troops. The

100-member guerilla force guarding the saltworks fled as the troops approached.[44]

The capture of the USS *Maple Leaf* was possibly the only Confederate engagement to occur in Princess Anne County after it became a federally occupied military district. The USS *Maple Leaf* sailed from Norfolk in early June 1863, enroute to Fort Delaware with 101 Confederate officers as prisoners. Just outside the Virginia Capes, the prisoners overpowered the crewmen and captured the steamer. One of the prisoners, Captain Fuller, had commanded a Confederate gunboat on the Mississippi River. He planned to sail the *Maple Leaf* to Nassau. The prisoners, however, discovered that there was not enough fuel for the voyage, so they beached the *Maple Leaf* south of Cape Henry and made their escape over land. Once the Union crew regained control of the steamer, they hurriedly returned to Fort Monroe to report the escape. Confederate prisoners left behind during the escape due to illness or severe wounds were sent to Fort Delaware.

The escapees pushed southward, obtaining food, directions, and advice at a remote farmhouse. They captured boats on Currituck Sound and crossed to Knott's Island, where the White family gave them food and shelter. The following day they crossed to the mainland near Currituck Courthouse, took to the swamps, and eventually met a Confederate guerilla who guided them to Richmond and safety. In the Confederate capital, these rebels were received as heroes and were given lodging in the Spotswood Hotel, the finest accommodation in the city.

When Mr. White returned to Knott's Island, the Federal cavalrymen were not far behind him. He fled into the woods and his wife took to her bed. The cavalrymen pillaged the farm and arrested White's ten-year-old daughter for aiding and abetting the Confederate prisoners.[45] She was imprisoned at the Pungo Ferry garrison.

After the Civil War, the citizens' pre-war prosperity was nearly impossible to recover. Lost fortunes were difficult to replenish in the stunted agricultural economy. The emancipated slaves lived on local farms and at Freedmen's Bureaus, which were established at Kempsville, on the Greenwich plantation, and at Rolleston, once the residence of Governor Henry A. Wise.[46] The military districts established during the war were replaced with a system of local government units in 1869.[47] Under the Reconstruction Acts, Virginia was readmitted to the Union in 1870.[48]

Notes for Chapter 9

1. Rogers Dey Whichard, *The History of Lower Tidewater Virginia*, vol. 1 (New York: Lewis Historical Publishing Company, Inc., 1959), 300-301.
2. William H. Stewart, *History of Norfolk County, Virginia, and Representative Citizens* (Chicago, Il.: Biographical Publishing Company, 1902), 35.
3. Whichard, vol 1, 301.
4. Stewart, 38.
5. Whichard, vol. 1, 302.
6. Stewart, 38.
7. Isaac S. Harrell, *Loyalism in Virginia* (Durham, N.C.: Duke University Press, 1926), 40-41.
8. Katherine Fontaine Syer, "The County of Princess Anne, 1691-1957" in *The History of Lower Tidewater Virginia*, vol. 2, ed. Rogers Dey Whichard (New York: Lewis Historical Publishing Company, Inc., 1959), 73.
9. Whichard, vol. 1, 301.
10. Harrell, 39.
11. Stewart, 38.
12. William P. Palmer and H.W. Flourney, *Calendar of Virginia State Papers and Other Manuscripts*, vol. 3 (Richmond, Va.: James E. Goode, 1881, 1890), 166-167.
13. Stewart, 35.
14. Ibid., 50.
15. Ibid., 35.
16. Palmer and Flourney, vol. 3, 166.
17. Harrell, 59.
18. B. D. White, "Gleanings in the History of Princess Anne County," in *An Economic and Social Survey of Princess Anne County*, ed. E.E. Ferebee and J. Pendleton Wilson, Jr. (Charlottesville, Va.: Michie Company, 1924), 15.
19. Edward Wilson James, *The Lower Norfolk County Virginia Antiquary*, vol. 1 (New York: Peter Smith, 1951), 9.
20. Ibid., vol 2, 133.
21. Sadie Scott Kellam and V. Hope Kellam, *Old Houses in Princess Anne Virginia* (Portsmouth, Va.: Printcraft, 1958), 193.
22. Syer, 76.
23. Palmer and Flourney, vol. 2, 542.
24. Ibid., vol. 2, 611.
25. Ibid., vol. 2, 626.
26. Ibid., vol. 3, 101.
27. Carolyn Caywood, "Battle Off the Virginia Capes," Virginia Beach Public Library, Spring 2006.
28. W. H. T. Squires, "Norfolk in By-Gone Days," *Norfolk Ledger Dispatch*, 11 March 1937, 16.
29. Ibid.
30. Syer, 84.
31. Stewart, 60-63.
32. Syer, 96-97.
33. John Fortier, *15th Virginia Cavalry* (Lynchburg, Va.: H. E. Howard, Inc., 1993), 2.
34. Michael A. Cavanaugh, *6th Virginia Infantry* (Lynchburg, Va.: H. E. Howard, Inc., 1988), 4-5.
35. Stewart Sifakis, *Compendium of the Confederate Armies: Virginia* (New York: Facts on File, Inc., 1992), 174-175.
36. Stephen S. Mansfield, *Princess Anne County and Virginia Beach: A Pictorial History* (Norfolk, Va.: The Donning Company/Publishers, 1989), 67.
37. N. E. Warriner, *A Register of Military Events in Virginia 1861-1865* (n.p.: Virginia Civil War Commission, 1959), 9.
38. "Another Scrap of History," *Norfolk Landmark*, 7 November 1879, 1.
39. Lenoir Chambers, "Notes on Life in Occupied Norfolk, 1862-1865," *The Virginia Magazine of History and Biography*, vol. 73, no. 2, April 1965, 132-135.
40. Robert N. Scott, *The War of Rebellion: A Compilation of the Official Records of the Union and Confederate Armies*, series 1, vol. 27, pt. 3 (Washington: Government Printing Office, 1889), 846.
41. Ibid., 846-849.
42. Ibid., 850-851.
43. Robert N. Scott, *The War of Rebellion: A Compilation of the Official Records of the Union and Confederate Armies*, series 1, vol. 29, pt. 1 (Washington: Government Printing Office, 1890), 143-144.
44. Ibid., 200.
45. W.H.T. Squires, "Norfolk in By-Gone Days," *Norfolk Ledger Dispatch*, 3 October 1935, 14.
46. White, 11-12.
47. Thomas C. Parramore, Peter C. Stewart, and Tommy L. Bogger, *Norfolk: The First Four Centuries* (Charlottesville, Va.: University of Virginia Press, 1994), 237-238.
48. "Virginia," *World Book Encyclopedia*, vol. 20 (Chicago, Il.: World Book,, Inc., 1996), 422.

Chapter 10

Lifesaving Stations and Shipwrecks

Between 1874 and 1915, more than 185 shipwrecks occurred along the Virginia coast.[1] The majority were due to rapid and violent changes in the weather, which caused ships to run aground or be stranded on sandbars.[2] During the 1870s, Congress authorized the construction of a network of lifesaving stations along the east coast in order to render assistance to ships in peril and to prevent loss of life.

Lifesaving District Six stretched from Cape Henry, Virginia, to Cape Fear, North Carolina. Five stations were built on the coast of Virginia in District Six. These were Cape Henry, Seatack, Dam Neck Mills, Little Island, and False Cape.[3] These stations served as a primary source of help for ships in distress until 1915, when the United States Coast Guard was formed.[4]

Each lifesaving station consisted of a sturdy, all-weather building with a lookout platform, a boat room, two surfboats, and various pieces of rescue equipment. The most popular lifesaving device was the breeches buoy, a cork life preserver with a pair of heavy canvas breeches attached. After an initial rope was sent to the vessel by a firing device, the breeches buoy was pulled to the ship. The endangered person would sit in the breeches with his legs hanging through and the life preserver at chest level. The lifesaving crew could then haul the buoy to safety by lines reaching from ship to shore.

Each station normally had a crew of six surfmen with a keeper in charge. Members of the crew were qualified men who lived in the vicinity of the station, manning it during the winter season, from December 1 to April 30. Each crew member was paid forty dollars per month.

At four designated times during every twenty-four hour period, two surfmen from each station would set off in opposite directions along the beach, looking for any evidence of ships needing assistance. They would meet patrols from adjoining stations, exchange information, and return to their assigned posts.[5]

The lifesaving stations also served as hospitals for survivors needing medical attention after a shipwreck. The rescued were provided with shelter, clothing, food, and other necessities. Each station had a small library of popular materials to help relieve the boredom of being stranded.[6]

Courtesy of City of Virginia Beach, VA ComIT Center for GIS

Lifesaving Stations of Virginia Beach

Cape Henry Lifesaving Station

One of the most spectacular rescues in lifesaving annals took place in 1906. According to a *Norfolk Virginian-Pilot* newspaper article dated March 1, 1906, the schooner *George M. Grant* ran aground on February 27 during a blinding snowstorm. The schooner was stranded 100 yards from the Cape Henry Lifesaving Station. Strong winds and raging seas made rescue by the lifesaving crew impossible. With darkness setting in, the ten men aboard the schooner seemed to be doomed, as the surfmen watched helplessly while the ship foundered in mast-high waves.

Suddenly, the tug *Jack Twohy* appeared on the horizon and was skillfully maneuvered by Captain Partridge through the treacherous seas, until his crew was able to secure a line to the *Grant*. Captain A. C. Pelton and his crew of nine men were quickly put on board, and the tug then pulled clear of the schooner and headed for port.

The tugboat crew members were highly praised for their daring and bravery, but Captain Partridge modestly commented that he did no more than any other man would have done under the circumstances. He was a cousin of the Captain[7] John Willis[8] Partridge who commanded the Seatack Lifesaving Station and who, with his lifesaving crew, was standing by on shore watching the rescue.[9]

On March 31, 1906, the Italian bark *Antonio* lost her bearings in a gale and became disabled off Cape Henry. All eleven crew members were rescued by surfboat and taken to the Cape Henry station to recuperate. The bark was bound from Uruguay to Alexandria, Virginia.[10]

Fog was a major cause of shipwrecks off the coast of Virginia. It was at times so thick that navigational aides were useless.[11] On October 20, 1906, gale-whipped seas and dense fog stranded the steamer *George Farwell* near Cape Henry. All aboard were rescued. According to a newspaper account, this rescue operation involved the use of a breeches buoy as a "baggage express." Not only was passenger Frederick S. Heitmann rescued, but so was his luggage. He had been on a voyage for his health and said, after this traumatic experience, that he was "cured of the sea."[12]

Courtesy of the Old Coast Guard Station

BREECHES BUOY RESCUE APPARATUS
Drawing by Julie J. Pouliot

Little Island Lifesaving Station

One of the most remote lifesaving stations was Little Island Lifesaving Station, now the location of Little Island City Park below Sandbridge.[13] Tragedy struck this station in 1887. It was snowing and bitterly cold in the early morning hours of January 8, when surfmen spotted the German ship *Elizabeth* stranded several hundred yards from shore. Rescue crews rushed from the Little Island and Dam Neck Mills station to help, but they were unable to get a line out to the ship. The decision was made to risk sending a lifeboat into the raging ocean as a final rescue attempt. The surfmen managed to reach the *Elizabeth* and took several of her men on board. They then headed for land along with the ship's lifeboat, which contained more of her crew members. As the two boats neared the shore, they both capsized in the surf.[14] For days afterwards, rescuers pulled frozen bodies from the sea.[15]

All members of the *Elizabeth's* crew perished. In addition, Captain Able Belanga, station crewman George Stone, John Land (all from Little Island), James Belanga, and Joseph Spratley (from Dam Neck Mills) lost their lives.[16] They were buried at Seaside Neck, West Neck, and Pungo Ridge. Two of the Little Island rescue party were saved. Frank Tedford was pulled from the surf nearly frozen and semiconscious, while John Etheridge was seriously injured.[17]

Dam Neck Mills Lifesaving Station

This station was built in the vicinity of two eighteenth-century corn and grain windmills which operated at Dam Neck. Captain Bailey Barco, who was in charge of the lifesaving station, bought one of the mills in 1880. The other mill was owned by David Malbon. The two mills stood approximately 250 yards apart and were about 300 yards from the ocean. Captain Barco's mill, severely damaged by an 1894 storm, was abandoned and never repaired.[18]

The windmills were not Dam Neck's only landmarks. The Chapel by the Sea, a mission of the Eastern Shore Chapel, was built there in the summer of 1889 with lumber salvaged from the wreck of the *Agnes Barton*.[19] This American brig ran aground near the Dam Neck Mills station during a storm on March 14, 1889. Four crewmen were rescued by breeches buoy before the buoy ceased moving and became unusable. By daylight the surfmen still found it impossible to reach the ship, and were unable to rescue the remaining crew members before the *Agnes Barton* sank.[20]

The *Henry B. Hyde* also became a landmark on the beach one-and-a-half miles south of the Dam Neck Mills station. The ship went aground twice on February 11, 1904, during a northeast blizzard. It was being towed by the tug *Brittania*, which cut it loose to avoid being wrecked herself. Captain Pearson, his wife, and crew were rescued. Attempts were made to refloat the ship several times. On September 16, the *Henry B. Hyde* was finally refloated, but broke in two on October 4.[21]

Since 1951, the site of the Dam Neck Mills Lifesaving Station, the eighteenth-century windmills, and the Chapel by the Sea has been the property of the United States Navy.[22]

Courtesy of the Mariners' Museum, Newport News, Virginia

THE *HENRY B. HYDE*
The ship was grounded off the Virginia Beach coast in 1904.

False Cape Lifesaving Station

The southernmost Virginia lifesaving station was False Cape Lifesaving Station, located in the area which is now False Cape State Park. The False Cape surfmen were involved in rescues of approximately fifty shipwrecks between 1875 and 1915.[23]

One of the most memorable of these wrecks took place in October of 1889 during a tremendous storm. The *Henry P. Simmons* was sailing from Charleston to Baltimore on October 23, when her heavy cargo of phosphate rock caused her to plunge in the rough ocean and take water aboard. The schooner sank one-and-a-half miles offshore near the Virginia-North Carolina border. By noon on October 24, the False Cape surfmen and other lifesaving station crew members had been unable to get a buoy line or a surfboat to the ship. The storm raged for five days and the ship continued to sink. On October 28, as the storm abated, a surfboat was finally dispatched to the *Henry P. Simmons.* Robert Lee Garnett was the only person rescued from the ship. The other seven crew members had fallen from the ship's rigging and drowned or died of exhaustion.[24]

Seatack Lifesaving Station

Of the five Virginia Beach lifesaving stations, probably the most famous was Seatack Lifesaving Station, built in 1878 at present day 24th Street and Atlantic Avenue. The name Seatack has been traced back to a combination of the words "sea" and "attack," possibly because of a British attack from the ocean in this area during the War of 1812. The name may also have originated due to the fact that ships sailing from the Chesapeake Bay often had to tack south along the coast before heading east to Europe.[25]

Courtesy of Raymond J. Lewis

Old Coast Guard Station, as seen today

The Seatack Station was a hub of growth for the Virginia Beach oceanfront resort area.[26] A new station was constructed near the site of the original building in 1903.[27] This newer building was decommissioned by the United States Coast Guard in 1969[28] and today houses the Old Coast Guard Station (formerly the Lifesaving Museum of Virginia).

Two of the best known shipwrecks on the coast of Virginia Beach occurred near the Seatack Station. One of them involved the four-masted schooner *Benjamin F. Poole*, which ran aground during a gale on April 7, 1889. The ship was disabled, but not ruined. Efforts to refloat her proved fruitless. The schooner rested on the beach, with Captain Charlton aboard, for seventeen months, a conversation piece for hotel guests and sightseers.

One of the sightseers was Matilda Lowhermueller, whom Captain Charlton courted and married in July 1890. They honeymooned on the vessel for three months until the *Poole* was finally refloated during a storm in the autumn of that year. The ship was repaired and remained in service for many years.[29]

Other mariners did not fare as well. The Norwegian bark *Dictator*, with the captain's wife and young son aboard, was bound from Pensacola, Florida, to England, carrying a cargo of yellow pine. She was damaged at sea by a series of storms. While heading for harbor in Hampton Roads during another gale, the *Dictator* ran aground approximately one mile north of the Seatack Station on March 27, 1891. Surfmen from both the Cape Henry and Seatack stations responded to the ship's distress.[30]

Because of a strong wind blowing toward land, the lifesaving crew's efforts to shoot a buoy line to the bark proved futile. The *Dictator*'s captain, Jorgen Jorgensen, was finally able to float an empty barrel ashore with a line attached. The lifesaving crew tied the breeches buoy to the line so those on the ship could haul it back. Before anyone could be rescued, however, the buoy line became entangled in the ship's rigging and the buoy was rendered useless. Four of the *Dictator*'s crew were able to reach shore in the ship's only usable boat, with instructions from Captain Jorgensen to send the boat back to the *Dictator*. However, Keeper Edward Drinkwater of the Seatack Station felt that neither the ship's small boat, nor a surfboat, could endure the journey to and from the *Dictator* and decided not to risk sending either. Instead, the breeches buoy was repaired and several more crew members were hauled ashore before the ship began to break apart. Among those left on board were Captain Jorgenson,

Courtesy of the Old Coast Guard Station

Original Norwegian Lady
This wooden figurehead was from the 1891 wreck of the *Dictator.*

his wife, Johanne (who was near hysteria and had refused to get into the breeches buoy), and their four-year-old son.

As the ship was being battered to pieces by mountainous waves, Captain Jorgensen and Seaman Jean Baptiste, in desperation, tossed a ladder overboard in the hope that the Jorgensens could cling to it and be washed ashore. Captain Jorgensen tied his son, Carl, to his chest and attempted to board the ladder but was swept away from it by the heavy surf. Carl was torn from his father's arms and drowned. Johanne, along with four others who remained aboard, also drowned as the *Dictator* was demolished. Captain Jorgensen made the journey to shore by holding to a piece of wreckage. Lifesaving crewmen found him later on the beach, exhausted and barely able to walk. Second Mate Andersen also survived.

Johanne Jorgensen's body was recovered two days later, and Carl Jorgensen was found after eight days. Both were buried in Elmwood Cemetery in Norfolk. The heartbroken Captain Jorgensen returned to Norway following the tragedy.[31] Years later, in 1912, he went back to sea as first officer of the Danish steamship *Pennsylvania*.[32]

Courtesy of Albert B. Cain

New Norwegian Lady
The bronze statue was dedicated on September 22, 1962.

After the wreck of the *Dictator*, her wooden figurehead washed ashore near the Princess Anne Hotel. Emily Gregory, a hotel guest, spotted it in the surf and pointed it out to the hotel manager, who had it retrieved from the ocean and set up on the beach.[33] The weathered figurehead, an elegant Scandanavian lady, stood on the oceanfront at 16th Street until 1953, when it was moved to the city garage in a state of disrepair.[34]

In 1960, Thomas Baptist, a summer resident from Arlington, Virginia, began work on a project to make the beloved "Norwegian Lady" a permanent memorial. He appealed to the city manager of Virginia Beach and to the Norwegian Embassy in Washington. Both received his idea with enthusiasm. Baptist wrote an article[35] entitled "The Story of a Norwegian Lady,"[36] which was well-publicized in Norway. The citizens of Moss, the *Dictator*'s home port, responded enthusiastically and raised the necessary funds to build matching bronze "Norwegian Lady" statues.[37]

Dedication ceremonies were held simultaneously in Virginia Beach and Moss[38] on September 22, 1962,[39] and the "Norwegian Lady" statues were unveiled. One stands at 25th Street in Virginia Beach and the other at the harbor at Moss, Norway, facing each other across the ocean.[40] The mission of the "Norwegian Lady" is displayed on a plaque attached to the front of the statue.

I Am
The Norwegian Lady
I Stand Here
As My Sister Before Me
To Wish All Men Of The Sea
Safe Return Home

Notes for Chapter 10

1. "Early Life Savers," Supplement to *Virginia Beach Beacon*, 21-24 February 1988, B26.
2. Richard A. Pouliot and Julie J. Pouliot, *Shipwrecks on the Virginia Coast and the Men of the United States Life-Saving Service* (Centreville, Md.: Tidewater Publishers, 1986), 23.
3. Ibid., 6-8.
4. Ibid., 153.
5. Ibid., 6-18.
6. Ibid., 41-42.
7. "Crew Rescued Out of Jaws of Death," *Norfolk Virginian-Pilot*, 1 March 1906, 1.
8. Meredith Holland (grandson of John Willis Partridge). Letter to Charlotte G. Irish, 27 June 1994. Courtesy of the Old Coast Guard Station, 7 March 1996.
9. "Crew Rescued Out of Jaws of Death."
10. "Italian Bark Antonio on Beach," *Norfolk Virginian-Pilot*, 1 April 1906, 5.
11. Pouliot, 156.
12. "Farwell's Crew Rescued in Darkness," *Norfolk Virginian-Pilot,* 23 October 1906, 1.
13. "Little Island Lifesaving Station," Supplement to *Virginia Beach Beacon,* 21-24 February 1988, B34.
14. "Disastrous Shipwreck," *Norfolk Landmark,* 9 January 1887, 1.
15. *Norfolk Landmark,* 11 January 1887, 1.
16. "Disastrous Shipwreck."
17. *Norfolk Landmark,* 11 January 1887, 1.
18. Louisa Venable Kyle, "Old Post Windmills of Virginia," *Commonwealth,* February 1956, 21, 44.
19. *The Dam Neck Story,* (Virginia Beach, Va.: Fleet Combat Training Center, 1988), Prepared under the direction of Captain H. E. Carroll II, n.p.
20. Pouliot, 76-78.
21. Ibid., 129-133.
22. *The Dam Neck Story.*
23. Pouliot, 160-177.
24. Ibid., 86-88.
25. Joseph W. Dunn Jr. and Barbara S. Lyle, *Virginia Beach: Wish You Were Here* (Norfolk, Va.: Donning Publishers, 1983), 19.
26. Pouliot, 155.
27. Stephen S. Mansfield, *Princess Anne County and Virginia Beach: A Pictorial History* (Norfolk, Va.: The Donning Company/Publishers, 1989), 81.
28. Ibid., 97.
29. Louisa Venable Kyle, "On the Benjamin F. Poole," *Virginian-Pilot and the Portsmouth Star,* 15 April 1956, 3C.
30. Pouliot, 94.
31. William O. Foss, *The Norwegian Lady and the Wreck of the Dictator* (Norfolk, Va.: Donning Company/Publishers, Inc., 1977), 26-42.
32. Ibid., 68.
33. Kay Doughtie Sewell, "An Old Man's Memories: Her Oldest Resident Recalls 71 Years of Virginia Beach," *Virginian-Pilot and the Portsmouth Star,* 25 March 1956, C1.
34. Katherine Fontaine Syer, "The Town and City of Virginia Beach," in *The History of Lower Tidewater, Virginia,* vol. 2, ed. Rogers Dey Whichard (New York: Lewis Historical Publishing Company, Inc., 1959), 128-129.
35. Mary Reid Barrow, "Norwegian Lady Statues: A Legacy That Means So Much to the Beach," *Virginia Beach Beacon,* 17 February 1993, 7.
36. Foss, 76.
37. Barrow, "Norwegian Lady Statues."
38. "Identical Statues Built on Opposite Shores," *Virginian-Pilot,* 15 June 1990, B3.
39. Barrow, "Norwegian Lady Statues."
40. Sam Martinette, "The Vikings Are Coming – But Just to Honor Norwegian Lady," *Virginian-Pilot,* 15 June 1990, B3.

Chapter 11

Virginia Beach: The Birth of a Resort

In the 1880s, a dynamic new chapter in Princess Anne history began. Colonel Marshall Parks, a prominent developer and entrepreneur, focused local attention on the area he is credited with naming "Virginia Beach." Colonel Parks and his investors organized the Norfolk and Virginia Beach Railroad and Improvement Company to acquire oceanfront property. He erected a wooden clubhouse at Seventeenth Street, which was the first structure in the area now known as the "resort strip."[1] In July 1883, railroad service from Norfolk to Virginia Beach began when Captain Virginius Freeman, engineer of the Virginia Beach Railroad, took a party of twenty-five men on the railcar's initial run. Colonel Park's shuttle steamer service operated out of his Norfolk pier terminal and traveled the Eastern Branch of the Elizabeth River to the Broad Creek terminal. From the Broad Creek terminal, the railroad ran to the oceanfront, a distance of fourteen miles.[2]

The train brought visitors to the oceanfront area. Many visitors stayed at the Virginia Beach Hotel, a small hostelry accommodating seventy-five guests. Located just south of Seventeenth Street at the oceanfront, the hotel opened in the early 1880s and was financed by Colonel Parks and a group of investors developing the area into a resort.[3]

The original clubhouse was moved to Eighteenth Street and Atlantic Avenue, where it was turned over to Mrs. Barton Meyers for use as an infant sanitarium.[4] The building was renovated and opened on June 6, 1888. Children came to the sanitarium for the fresh air and therapeutic ocean breezes, as well as for free medical treatment. A nurse and a matron were hired to care for the children. The staff, buildings and medical treatment were paid for by donations from Norfolk and Princess Anne County citizens. The Virginia Beach Railroad offered free passes for train transportation to parents taking their children to the infant sanitarium.[5]

Colonel Parks and his associates in the railroad company did not fare well with their investments. On May 17, 1887, the hotel, pavilion, railroad, and 1,500 acres of beachfront land were put up for public auction, according to a decree of the court. The sum of $170,000 (approximately $3.5 million in 2006 dollars) was the highest bid, and the buildings and property were sold to Mr. C. W. Mackey of Pittsburgh, Pennsylvania. Mr. Mackey served on the board of directors of the Norfolk and Virginia Beach Railroad and Improvement Company.[6] Under new management, and with noticeable improvements, the Virginia Beach Hotel and Pavilion reopened on June 6, 1887, for the summer season.[7]

Courtesy of the Sargeant Memorial Room, Norfolk Public Libraries

Wooden Boardwalk, 1888

The following year, the hotel was renamed the Princess Anne Hotel, opening for the summer season on June 1, 1888. The newspaper announcement in the *Public Ledger* called it "a magnificent hotel...with electric lights...an elevator...bath houses with a veranda...a good ballroom," among other improvements. On the roof of the hotel were three large tanks to supply water in case of a fire.[8] The fire safety equipment would become extremely important as the hotel entered the twentieth century.

The upgrades to the hotel made by C. W. Mackey's newly reorganized Virginia Beach Improvement Company totaled $250,000, a huge sum for 1889. A winter season, beginning in mid-February, was added to entice clientele from the north, and a New York office was opened to handle accommodations. The company also proposed to substitute standard track for the narrow gauge railroad.[9]

Courtesy of the Sargeant Memorial Room, Norfolk Public Libraries

Princess Anne Hotel, circa 1907

By 1888, the property adjacent to the hotel had been subdivided and lots were offered for sale to the public. A number of prominent citizens purchased property and began building cottages. Among the owners of the first cottages were Colonel Lucien D. Starke, Judge F. M. Whitehurst, Judge Robert Hughes, Floyd Hughes, A. S. Taylor, C.A. Woodard, Merritt Cooke, Barton Meyers, and Bishop Beverly D. Tucker.[10]

The Princess Anne Hotel stretched from Fourteenth to Sixteenth streets. First-class bands and artists performed in the ballroom, attracting large crowds. Other amenities of the hotel included a post office, a Western Union Telegraph office, and telephone service. Besides being praised for its healthy sea air and surf, the hotel also promoted its exclusive Atlantic beach location near an extensive forest that tempered cold north winds in the winter. The Princess Anne Hotel could accommodate 400 guests.[11]

Distinguished visitors and celebrities frequented the hotel, including Presidents Benjamin Harrison and Grover Cleveland, and Vice-President Levi P. Morton. One guest remarked about three young people "careening madly around the dance pavilion" when describing the Barrymores – John, Ethel, and Lionel. Other prominent visitors to the Princess Anne Hotel were Alexander Graham Bell, Cyrus Field, who laid the first transatlantic cable, and the McCormick family of Chicago, famous for their invention of the reaper and other farming equipment.[12]

Sadly, the fashionable hotel was completely destroyed by fire in the early morning hours of June 10, 1907. Sergeant Carl Boeschen, of the Richmond Light Artillery Blues, was hurrying to the depot to board the first train for Norfolk to attend the Jamestown Exposition, when he saw smoke and flames coming from the hotel's kitchen roof and alerted the occupants. The guests escaped with only their nightclothes.

The loss, estimated at $125,000, could have been much worse since there was no fire-fighting equipment at the oceanfront. A waterworks system, including hydrants and an 80,000 gallon holding tank, was to have been in operation the next day; however, these provisions were not completed in time to save the hotel. At the time of the fire, nearly twenty women residents and hotel guests formed a bucket brigade that saved the surrounding buildings from destruction.[13]

The resort community was incorporated as the town of Virginia Beach in March, 1906.[14] Other businesses had been flourishing prior to the town's incorporation. The first grocery store opened in 1897. The store's proprietor, J. W. Bonney, was the first of the Seventeenth Street merchants. This profitable venture was soon followed by a drugstore, a hardware store, and several general stores.[15]

Although not as grand as the Princess Anne Hotel, there were other early hotels offering modest accommodations at the oceanfront: Ocean View, Arlington, and Breakers. Houses and cottages continued to spring up along the beach. B. P. Holland, a pioneer resident of Virginia Beach and its first mayor, postmaster, and telegrapher, built his second home on the west-side of Atlantic Avenue in 1908. Holland had built the resort's first brick year-round home for his new bride in 1895. This house, located on Twelfth Street at the oceanfront, was sold to the DeWitt family in 1909. Called *Wittenzand,* a Dutch word meaning "white sand," the household saw much activity as the family filled the residence with ten children.[16]

The town hall, built in 1907, housed the volunteer fire department, the first school, and the jail.[17] Thomas J. Warden was the first policeman in Virginia Beach, and served as chief of police for the town.[18]

The amusement complex known as Seaside Park, spanning from Thirty-first to Thirty-third streets, opened in 1912. Built by Norfolk and Southern Railroad, the facility was eventually leased by the Laskin family in the 1920s.[19] The "Old Casino," as it was called, featured a salt-water pool, bathhouses, a restaurant, amusement concessions, and the Peacock Ballroom. The Peacock was "the place to go" in the 1920s and 1930s. Charging ten cents a dance set (five or six dances) or three sets for a quarter, the Peacock Ballroom boasted such dance band greats as Paul Whiteman, Cab Calloway, Duke Ellington, and Fred Waring.[20] A fire in 1955 destroyed most of the Old Casino. Seaside Amusement Park was rebuilt in the years following the fire. A popular entertainment spot through the 1960s and 1970s, the park was sold in 1981, and the attractions dismantled.[21] The 291-room Thirty-first Street Hilton Hotel, featuring a parking garage, two restaurants with oceanfront views, and numerous specialty shops, now occupies the property.[22]

The Princess Anne Country Club at Thirty-eighth Street and Pacific Avenue was the resort's first country club, incorporated in 1916. Ninety-five acres of land were donated by a real estate syndicate for a golf course and clubhouse. The area was such a wilderness that mosquitoes and water moccasins were a major problem in clearing the land in the course's early years of play. The eighteen-hole course was designed by John M. Baldwin, with the assistance of Walter Becket, the professional golfer at the Norfolk Country Club. President Warren G. Harding made an historic visit to play the course in 1921.[23]

James M. Jordan, Jr., the club's youngest charter member, had the distinction of being the first man to ride a surfboard on the East Coast. Jordan's uncle, Walter F. Irvin, gave him the Hawaiian-made surfboard as a gift in 1912. The redwood board stood nine feet tall and weighed 110 pounds.[24]

The Princess Anne Country Club added a touch of elegance and sophistication to the area, drawing members of high society to the beach. Affluent society members were also attracted by the opening of the exclusive and luxurious Cavalier Hotel in 1927. Located on Forty-second Street and Atlantic Avenue, the Cavalier Hotel began in 1924 as a community project to foster the growth of Virginia Beach. The Virginia Beach Resort and Hotel Corporation[25] financed the $2 million project. When the Cavalier Hotel opened its doors, paying guests called it the "Queen of the Beach." Governor Harry F. Byrd raved, "Virginia has the best resort hotel in America!" The hotel boasted 226 rooms, a barbershop, confectionery, hot and

Courtesy of the Old Coast Guard Station

Battered Concrete Boardwalk and Coast Guard Station,
after the Ash Wednesday storm, March 7, 1962

cold taps at every sink, with an extra spigot for iced water, Perma-Kote washable wallpaper, china service in the restaurant depicting the planting of the first cross on Virginia soil, silk damask hangings in the ballroom, and an 1,875 ft.² heated pool. Famous guests included F. Scott and Zelda Fitzgerald, Fatty Arbuckle, golfer Sam Snead, Snooky Lanson, and Victor Borge.[26]

The original wooden boardwalk at the oceanfront was built in 1888 and stretched southward from the Princess Anne Hotel. Most of it was destroyed in the hotel fire of 1907. Work began on a new concrete boardwalk in 1926, when the Virginia Beach Walkway Corporation agreed to underwrite the town's $250,000 bond issue.

Two wooded bulkheads were added to the concrete structure in 1938 and 1939, extending the boardwalk to the Cavalier Hotel.[27] The concrete boardwalk sustained serious damage in the Ash Wednesday storm of March 7, 1962, when twenty to thirty-foot waves battered the seawall.[28]

A unique attraction drawing visitors to Virginia Beach is the Association for Research and Enlightenment. The original building housing the collected readings of Edgar Cayce, a nationally-known psychic, was built in 1919, and was later sold during the Depression. In 1956, the Association repurchased it. This building, and the new one next to it housing the library and educational facilities, is located at Sixty-seventh Street and Atlantic Avenue.[29] The Association for Research and Enlightenment currently has 33,000 members worldwide.[30]

The boardwalk and the resort area host a number of exciting events. The first Boardwalk Art Show was held in 1956 by the Virginia Beach Art Association. The outdoor show and sale is the longest enduring event in the city.[31] The four-day show features arts and crafts displays in tented booths, food, and live music in the evenings. The Boardwalk Art Show and Festival has become a leading outdoor art show in the United States with 300 artists and more than 250,000 visitors each year.[32]

Another tradition on the boardwalk is the Neptune Festival, held every September since 1974. Musical performers, aerial displays, food booths, fireworks, and an art show are events associated with the festival. It has been likened to Mardi Gras, with the crowning of King Neptune each year.[33] The Neptune Festival is one of the country's top 100 festivals and is a top ten festival event on the East Coast. Attended by an average of 400,000 people each year, the event generates hundreds of thousands of dollars in direct taxes to the city.[34]

Since 1962, the East Coast Surfing Championships have been considered "the locals' end-of-the-summer bash."[35] Sponsored by the Virginia Beach Jaycees, the event features musical performances by national and local artists, skateboarding, volleyball, and competitive and recreational running events, along with the surfing competition itself. Surfers from all over the United States compete in the tournament. Funds from the event are used to support various local charitable and community-building projects.[36]

The oceanfront area of Virginia Beach is a favorite of visitors and year-round residents alike. Remembering its history as a vital and exciting vacation spot, the beach continues to be the holiday destination of numerous tourists and a beloved home to thousands of "locals."

Notes for Chapter 11

1. Stephen S. Mansfield, *Princess Anne County and Virginia Beach: A Pictorial History* (Norfolk, Va.: The Donning Company, 1989), 77-78.
2. "A Splendid Road Soon to be Opened," *Public Ledger*, 17 July 1883, 1.
3. "Marshall Parks Dead," *Norfolk Landmark*, 12 June 1900, 2.
4. "An Important Movement," *Public Ledger*, 26 April 1888, 1.
5. "The Infant Hospital," *Public Ledger*, 2 June 1888, 1.
6. "Sale of the Virginia Beach Railroad," *Public Ledger*, 17 May 1887, 1.
7. "Local Sorts," *Public Ledger*, 6 June 1887, 1.
8. "Opening of the Princess Anne Hotel," *Public Ledger*, 2 June 1888, 1.
9. "Tidewater Virginia—Its Sanitary Advantages," *Norfolk Landmark*, 20 May 1888, 1.
10. "Norfolk's Winter Resort." *Norfolk Landmark*, 13 March 1889, 1.
11. "Improvements at Virginia Beach," *Public Ledger,* 28 April 1888, 1.
12. Kay Doughtie Sewell, "An Old Man's Memories: Her Oldest Resident Recalls 71 Years at Virginia Beach," *The Virginian-Pilot and the Portsmouth Star*, 25 March 1956, C1.
13. "Princess Anne Prey of Flames: Two Lives Lost," *Virginian-Pilot*, 11 June 1907, 1.
14. City of Virginia Beach, *Reconnaissance Level Phase I Architectural Survey Report* (Staunton, Va.: Frazier Associates, July 1992), 16.
15. "Virginia Beach: Gay Arrival in Dominion Annals," *Norfolk Virginian Pilot* (75th Anniversary Edition), 1940, n.p.
16. Louisa Venable Kyle, "Old Virginia Beach Keeps Identity," *Virginian-Pilot*, 24 August 1952, Section 4, 1.
17. "Virginia Beach: Gay Arrival in Dominion Annals."
18. James J. Jordan IV and Frederick S. Jordan, *Virginia Beach: A Pictorial History* (Richmond, Va.: Hale Publishing, 1975), 84.
19. Mansfield, 122.
20. Ruby Jean Phillips, "Seaside Park Holds Many Fond Memories," *Virginia Beach Beacon Visitors Guide,* 12 August 1973, v3.
21. Joseph V. Phillips, "Seaside Park Sold: Closing in 2 Years," *Virginian-Pilot,* 2 February 1981, D1, D3.
22. Marisa Taylor, "The 31st Street Hilton opened its Doors Thursday," *Virginian-Pilot*, 25 March 2005, from NewsBank database America's Newspapers, accessed 11/03/2005.
23. Kay Doughtie Sewell, "Out of a Dense Wilderness—Club and a Golf Course," *Virginian-Pilot*, 27 January 1957, C1.
24. Jordan, 109.
25. Ibid., 143.
26. William Ruehlmann, "Queen of the Beach," *Ledger-Star*, 24 June 1981, B1.
27. "Virginia Beach: Gay Arrival in Dominion Annals."
28. Jordan, 180.
29. Helen Crist, "ARE Library before Planners Tuesday," *Beacon*, 12 August 1973, 1, 6-7.
30. Larry Bonko, "History Channel Looking at Cayce," *Virginian-Pilot*, 7 August 2005, from NewsBank database America's Newspapers, accessed 11/03/2005.
31. Marlene Ford, "Now in Its 32nd Year, Art Show is Bigger, Better Than Ever," *Virginia Beach Beacon*, 18 June 1987, 19.
32. Stacy Parker, "Boardwalk Show Veteran to Return for 25th Year," *Virginian-Pilot*, 16 June 2005, from NewsBank database America's Newspapers, accessed 11/28/2005.
33. Pam Starr, "New Neptune King Learning to be Royal," *Virginia Beach Beacon*, 17 March 1995, 4.
34. "Virginia Beach Neptune Festival 2005," www.neptunefestival.com/history.htm, accessed 10/30/2005.
35. Lee Tolliver, "'Fantastic Weekend' for Surfing Bash," *Virginia Beach Beacon*, 31 August 1994, 12.
36. Lee Tolliver, "East Coast Surfing Championships Run Through Sunday at Oceanfront," *Virginian-Pilot*, 25 August 2004, from NewsBank database America's Newspapers, accessed 11/28/2005.

Chapter 12

Transportation

The advent of the railroads linking remote areas of Princess Anne County literally put Virginia Beach on the map. The Norfolk and Virginia Beach Railway inaugurated rail service to the beach on July 17, 1883. Norfolk and Southern took over the line in 1900. The improved railway was widened and branched to the south.

A rival railroad, the Chesapeake Transit Company, was formed in 1902. This company laid a standard gauge track from Norfolk, north to Cape Henry. The Chesapeake Transit Company's use of electric trains prompted Norfolk and Southern to modernize. Between 1902 and 1904, Norfolk and Southern replaced its narrow gauge track with standard gauge lines. Soon after, the company underwent reorganization and several name changes, and ultimately became known as Norfolk Southern. Later in 1904, Norfolk Southern bought out the Chesapeake Transit Company and consolidated the single track route.

The line was expanded with trains traveling in both directions, although not at the same time, as only a single track capable of one-way "traffic" remained.[1] This was known as the loop route, creating a continuous electric loop of traffic from Norfolk to the resort, then back to Norfolk by way of Cape Henry. By 1906, sixteen passenger trains a day made the journey between Norfolk and the beach.[2]

A branch line ran from Euclid Junction, near today's Witchduck Road. This line continued south to Princess Anne Courthouse, Pungo, and Munden Point. The Munden Point ferry carried passengers down the North Landing River to eastern North Carolina. The line eventually was shortened to stop at Back Bay.

The southern route had several nicknames. During the week, the route was called the "Courthouse Special," because the train took lawyers to and from court sessions at the Princess Anne Courthouse. On weekends, the Munden Point line was dubbed the "Sportsman's Special." It carried hunters and fishermen to the Back Bay area to try

Norfolk, Virginia Beach & Southern Railroad Co.

RUNNING BETWEEN NORFOLK AND

The — Famous VIRGINIA BEACH Sea-side Resort.

TIME-TABLE No. 1

In Effect Monday, February 1st, 1897, at 6:00 A. M.

DAILY, EXCEPT SUNDAY.

LEAVE NORFOLK.		ARRIVE VIRGINIA BEACH	LEAVE VIRGINIA BEACH.		ARRIVE NORFOLK.
7.00 a. m.	Mixed	8.00 a. m.	9.00 a. m.	Local Express	9.45 a. m.
9.20 a. m.	Through Express	9.55 a. m.	11.00 a. m.	Mixed	12.00 noon.
12.25 p. m.	Local Express	1.10 p. m.	2.15 p. m.	Local Express	3.00 p. m.
3.30 p. m.	Local Express	4.15 p. m.	4.45 p. m. (Stops only at Oceana, Lynnhaven and Kempsville)	Local Express	5.25 p. m.
6.15 p. m.	Local Express	7.00 p. m.	7.15 p. m.	Local Express	8.00 p. m.

SUNDAY TRAINS.

9.20 a. m. (Stops only at Kempsville, Lynnhaven and Oceana)		9.55 a. m.	10.10 a. m.	Local Express	10.55 a. m.
1.00 p. m.	Local Express	1.45 p. m.	2.15 p. m.	Local Express	3.00 p. m.
3.30 p. m.	Local Express	4.15 p m.	4.45 p. m. (Stops only at Oceana, Lynnhaven and Kempsville)		5.25 p. m.

All trains stop at Brambleton.
Trains stop only on signal at intermediate stations to put off or take on passengers. Through Express Trains make the trip in thirty-five minutes; Local Express Trains forty-five minutes.
A Chair Car is attached to Passenger trains. Seats 25 cents each.

B. P. HOLLAND, General Supt.

Courtesy of Edgar T. Brown

Time-Table No. 1
In 1897 passengers traveled from Norfolk to Virginia Beach for only 25¢.

---

their luck in rural Princess Anne County.[3] Fresh produce from the "lower country" also traveled this branch line north to be sold at markets and retail establishments.

Excursion trains ran all summer for residents who wanted to enjoy a day at the beach. Sunday schools from all over Tidewater had their yearly church picnics at the beach pavilions of Seaside Park, Chesapeake Beach, Cape Henry, and Ocean Park. Known as the "One-Step Special" or the "Two-Step Special" were the "Dance Trains," that carried young people to the casino for dancing each evening.

It was rare for accidents to disrupt service on the commuter line, however, a few incidents did occur. The worst accident happened on the morning of April 25, 1912, when an express train from the beach hit a freight engine. While there were no fatalities, many of the school children and businessmen aboard were injured. A snowstorm on March 3, 1927, caused another kind of disruption in service. Passengers returning home from work in Norfolk were stranded overnight on the train, which could no longer run in the deep snow.[4]

By the turn of the century, the popularity of railroads was waning, and the automobile began its reign as the supreme mode of transportation. As early as February 1904, newspapers carried stories of a spring racing tournament planned for the beachfront. New York automobile enthusiast Lee Strauss spurred interest in the coastal race, hoping to enlist the support of other "automobilists" of the era, such as Barney Oldfield and W. K. Vanderbilt. The original course considered was a fifty-mile stretch of shoreline, beginning in Virginia Beach, and extending south to Cape Hatteras.[5]

A fourteen-mile course, extending from below the Princess Anne Hotel to the wreck of the *Henry B. Hyde* and back, had been chosen for the September 5, 1904, event.[6] The Virginia Beach course was deemed even better than the one at Ormond/Daytona Beach, Florida, due to its hardness, smoothness, distance, and width.[7]

After six months of planning, the much anticipated beachfront automobile race was canceled. Overcast skies, a blinding mist, and thundering surf along the storm-swept shore "made it evident" early in the day "that no room would be left on the beach for the automobile races."[8]

Courtesy of the *Virginian-Pilot,* July 30, 1921

Opening of Virginia Beach Boulevard, the first concrete road from Norfolk to Virginia Beach

The popularity of automobiles grew from the turn of the century onward, necessitating the building of roads. In 1907, the railway was the primary means of transportation, and the only road from Norfolk to Virginia Beach was a treacherous dirt road that was difficult to travel.[9] Paths graveled with shells were the first type of roads built into Norfolk, with the first concrete roads in Virginia Beach being laid in 1913.[10]

July 29, 1921, saw the opening of Virginia Beach Boulevard, the first concrete, hard-surfaced road from Norfolk to Virginia Beach. The brief dedication ceremony drew 1,500 spectators, and 500 cars took part in the parade from Norfolk to the beach. Flags, signs, and ribbons festooned homes and businesses along the route. The concessions at the "Old Casino" were opened for free, and the exclusive Princess Anne Country Club welcomed the general public into their new clubhouse. A banquet was held at the Princess Anne Country Club for the officials responsible for the opening of Virginia Beach Boulevard and the planning of the day's festivities. These dignitaries included Alex P. Grice, chairman of the committee, and John A. Lessner, president of the Tidewater Automobile Association.[11]

The 1930s brought a decline in the use of trains. The ravaging economic effects of the Depression, along with the advent of the Model A Ford, proved to be adversaries of the railroads. To combat the trend, Norfolk Southern bought new AFC Brill railcars and began the Norfolk-Virginia Beach Railbus in 1935. The rail buses were like streetcars, modern, sleek, luxurious, quiet, and fast. They could travel at fifty-miles per hour.

During World War II, the rail bus provided the convenience of mass transit. Because of war priorities and shortages, however, the railroad could not maintain or modernize its equipment. Norfolk Southern discontinued its rail bus service in 1947. The northern and southern routes were torn up to make room for the expansion of roads in the resort area, namely the construction of Pacific Avenue.[12] Since 2002, activity on most of the track has stopped.[13]

Interest in a Norfolk-to-Virginia Beach commuter rail service is the subject of continued debate. A brief flurry of attention surrounded the concept of a Norfolk-Virginia Beach monorail system as early as the 1950s. The tracks of the east-west line ran in a nearly straight line from downtown Norfolk to the vicinity of 9th Street at the oceanfront.[14] A major effort was made in 1989 to bring a light rail, trolley-type system into service by Tidewater Regional Transit and their governing organization, the Tidewater Transportation District

Commission. Area city councils were divided in giving their support to the project, and the proposed light rail plan died.[15]

A major feat of engineering is located in the Bayside area of the city. The Chesapeake Bay Bridge Tunnel, which opened April 15, 1964, took 3 ½ years and $200 million to build.[16] The 17 ½ mile combination of trestles, bridges, and tunnels, links Chesapeake Beach to Wise Point on the Eastern Shore.[17] The Chesapeake Bay Bridge Tunnel is well-traveled, with an average number of 3.5 million vehicles annually.[18]

Traffic congestion has been an ongoing problem in Virginia Beach for several decades. According to the Hampton Roads Planning District Commission and the City of Norfolk, daily traffic volumes rose more than 16% along Interstate 264 and Virginia Beach Boulevard between 1995 and 2002. Further rapid growth is predicted, with a limited ability to expand roadways due to current physical constraints.[19] A 2005 transportation research report ranked Interstate 64 in Southeast Virginia as "the second worst summer traffic bottleneck in the nation."[20] With an estimated 2.5 to 4 million visitors to the Virginia Beach area each year,[21] traffic issues are a constant concern.

Notes for Chapter 12

1. Brown Carpenter, "Dead Beach Rail Links Recalled," *Ledger-Star,* 25 January 1974, A7.
2. Carl Craft and Nell Craft, "When Trains Made Tracks for the Beach," *Virginian-Pilot,* 27 July 1975, C5.
3. *Ledger-Star,* 25 January 1974, A7.
4. *Virginian-Pilot,* 27 July 1975, C5.
5. "Lee Strauss, the Well-Known New York Enthusiast, Is in Town and Will Meet Virginia Sportsmen This Afternoon," *Virginian-Pilot,* 12 February 1904, l2.
6. "Autos Will Speed on Beach for Trophies," *Virginian-Pilot,* 4 September 1904, l2.
7. *Virginian-Pilot,* 12 February 1904, l2.
8. "Celebration at Virginia Beach," *Virginian-Pilot,* 6 September 1904, 2.
9. Pat Roebuck, "Gettel Remembers Beach Progress in Terms of Days Railroading," *Beacon,* 30 July 1970, 23.
10. "Virginia Beach: Gay Arrival in Dominion Annals," *Norfolk Virginian-Pilot,* (75th Anniversary Edition), 1940, n.p.
11. "500 Automobiles in Parade Opening VA Beach Road," *Virginian-Pilot,* 30 July 1921, l4.
12. *Ledger-Star,* 25 January 1974, A7.
13. Carolyn Shapiro, "Norfolk Southern: Railroad Seeks to End Use of Its Norfolk-Beach Line," *Virginian-Pilot,* 6 June 2003, from NewsBank database America's Newspapers, accessed 10/31/2005.
14. Jim Henderson, "Revival of Beach-Norfolk Commuter Rail Sought," *Virginian-Pilot,* 9 August 1971, B1.
15. Mike Knepler, "Councils Track Future of Light Rail," *Virginian-Pilot,* 19 February 1989, B1.
16. Nigel Hawkes, *Structures: The Way Things Are Built* (New York: Macmillan Publishing Company, 1990), 232.
17. Don Hill, "Traffic Rolls Across Bay," *Virginian-Pilot,* 16 April 1964, 1, 10.
18. Tom Holden, "Bay Bridge May Offer Link to Build Road Projects," *Virginian-Pilot,* 17 June 2005, B1, from NewsBank database America's Newspapers, accessed 10/31/2005.

19. Norfolk LRT Project, "Final Environmental Impact Statement – Purpose and Need," Hampton Roads Transit, 1-11, http://www.hrtransit.org/lrt/FEIS/Chapter1/Chapter1.pdf, accessed 01/10/2006.

20. Steve Stone, "Tough Travels for Tourists in the Region," *Virginian-Pilot*, 1 July 2005, from NewBank database America's Newspapers, accessed 10/31/2005.

21. "Area Overviews," *Insiders' Guide to Virginia Beach*, 1st Edition, www.insiders.com/vabeach/main-overviews2.htm, accessed 11/06/2005.

Chapter 13

The Military

Although no bombs fell on Hampton Roads during the two World Wars, the fear of attack was an ever present reality. That vulnerable situation and proximity to strategic targets was a major reason for the construction of military installations in the region. In addition, the natural terrain of Tidewater, the Chesapeake Bay, and the surrounding waterways contributed to the establishment of military forces in the area.

Military aviation began on the Tidewater peninsula in the early 1920s. Test bombings were conducted to evaluate battle readiness over the summer of 1921. In July of that year, aviators sank former German warships, the *Frankfurt* and the *Ostfreisland*, in the joint army and navy exercises off the Virginia capes. Scores of military and national government officials witnessed these tests of potential air power.[1]

Twenty years later, the escalation of World War II and the increased need for air bases prompted the navy to acquire a 330-acre tract of land near Oceana for an auxiliary airfield.[2] In February of 1941, 272 acres near Creeds was acquired for an additional airfield.[3] One month later, a third tract of land, 441 acres northeast of Pungo, was obtained for naval airplane landing sites.[4]

With the anticipation of war, military personnel, defense workers, and their families poured into the area. By the end of 1940, the only homes available were unheated cottages at the beach, and the housing situation only got worse.[5]

The State Planning Board, in cooperation with the Hampton Roads Defense Council, conducted a housing survey in the area from April 1940 to May 1941. Results indicated that the population of the Southside, including Norfolk and Princess Anne County, had increased by 23 percent.[6] To help cope with the housing shortage, the navy commandeered several resort hotels, including the Cavalier and the Nansemond, for the duration of the war.[7] The Tidewater Hotel Association advertised in out-of-town newspapers for tourists to stay at home until the war ended. The area was subject to blackouts, beaches were closed after dark, and guest rooms were not available.[8]

Visitors were discouraged by the threat of the enemy lurking in the waters off the coast. German submarines operating off Cape Henry sank eight vessels in 1942 alone.[9] Oil slicks and debris continually washed ashore. On the afternoon of June 15, 1942, crowds of beachgoers heard an underwater explosion and witnessed two tankers sinking five miles from shore.[10] The last reported submarine attack off Cape Henry occurred on April 18, 1945, with the sinking of the steamship *Swiftscout.*[11]

Today, four military installations are based in Virginia Beach. They are located at Fort Story, Oceana, Dam Neck, and Little Creek. The oldest and most historic of these is Fort Story.

Fort Story

In the early 1900s, citizens and businessmen believed that a military installation was needed at Cape Henry as a first line of defense against an attack. Henry T. Trice, secretary of the Virginia Industrial Commission, proposed studies to convince the War Department and the federal government that "billions of dollars worth of property lying in an unprotected state within the Virginia capes" could be easily accessed "by an enemy in time of hostilities."[12] In 1913, President William Howard Taft signed an appropriations bill to purchase land at Cape Henry. The $8 million facility was named for General John P. Story, a Virginia-born general and artillery expert.[13]

During World War I, Fort Story was called "the American Gibraltar," and was considered to have the heaviest armament of any fort on the Atlantic Coast.[14] Soon after it was established, the fort expanded as additional acreage was acquired through the purchase of condemned properties around the facility. In 1940, the War Department granted the army use of 694 acres of Seashore State Park, inciting protests from civilians, scientists, and nature lovers. Outrage rang out at the army's apparent violation of the park's virgin wilderness.[15] Also angering many citizens was the beachfront location of the fort's hospital. The hospital site was later moved inland to save the shore's natural features and scenery.[16]

Fort Story's varied terrain provided excellent training grounds. Beginning in 1940, the facility served as a training site for World War II soldiers.[17] At one time, Fort Story was the location of a NIKE-Hercules guided missile site.[18]

Courtesy of the Sargeant Memorial Room, Norfolk Public Libraries

World War II – Fort Story
Photo by H. D. Vollmer, 1944

Scenic Fort Story also features the Cape Henry Memorial Cross. It marks the place where the first settlers arrived in the area on April 26, 1607.[19] In 1935, the large stone cross was erected amidst the sand dunes at Cape Henry to commemorate the first landing of the adventurers who went on to establish the first permanent English settlement in the New World at Jamestown on May 13, 1607. The landing cross is the site of an annual celebration and pilgrimage conducted by The Order of Cape Henry, 1607 on the Sunday nearest to April 26.

The first lighthouse authorized by the federal government sits at Fort Story. It began operation in 1792, and remained a vital beacon until 1881, when a new Cape Henry lighthouse was completed.[20]

The fort is still a very active facility today. Fort Story is the army's only Logistics-Over-The-Shore (LOTS) training and test site and is the army's only salt water purification training site. Fort Story is also used by navy and marine tenants, and periodically for active and reserve army, navy, marine, and air force units. Approximately 1,500 military and civilian personnel currently are based at Fort Story.[21]

Oceana

Plans for another Virginia Beach installation, the Oceana Air Station, began as early as 1938. Investigations were conducted for building an auxiliary landing field on acreage near Oceana and the Princess Anne Courthouse. Construction began in 1941, with a 2,500-foot runway and a wooden frame building, which served as an ambulance garage and caretaker's office.

Courtesy of the Public Affairs Office, Naval Air Station (NAS) Oceana

F/A-18F Super Hornet
A fighter, based at NAS Oceana

The attack on Pearl Harbor stepped up construction deadlines and provided the impetus for building better facilities. The station was commissioned on August 17, 1943, and remained in active status through World War II and the Korean War. In 1950, an expansion extended four runaways to 8,000 feet, making the facility a master jet base. The station was designated a naval air station on April 1, 1952, and officially was dedicated as Naval Air Station Oceana in June 1957.[22]

NAS Oceana began over sixty years ago on 328 acres of swampland.[23] As the navy's East Coast master jet base, the facility spans 6,000 acres and is the workplace of nearly 12,000 military and civilian personnel.[24] Oceana is home to sixteen fighter squadrons, two squadrons of F-14 Tomcats, and thirteen squadrons of F/A-18 Hornets and F/A-18 Super Hornets.

A round of BRAC (Base Realignment and Closure) Commission hearings occurred in 2005. It was decided that NAS Oceana would remain open, but only if certain conditions specified by the federal government were met. The major issue focused on the presence of approximately 3,400 homes and an unknown number of businesses in crash zones around the facility. Whether the City of Virginia Beach would buy and condemn these properties, or if another solution could be found was still pending in the autumn of 2005.[25]

Dam Neck

In the southern part of the city is the military facility Dam Neck, named for a lifesaving station established on that spot in the late 1800s. At that time, the site was a deserted beach near two post-type grain windmills known as Dam Neck Mills. Called the Fleet Air Defense Training Center, Dam Neck was first organized as an antiaircraft school in the beginning of World War II. Later, it was increased in size to accommodate Korean War operations. Military personnel are trained in the operation and maintenance of missiles at Dam Neck's Naval Guided Missiles School.[26]

Dam Neck is a part of Naval Air Station (NAS) Oceana, and the facility is known officially as the Atlantic Fleet Combat Training Center. It covers over 1,000 acres of marshes, sand dunes, and coastal beaches in southern Virginia Beach. Over 5,600 instructors, students, and support staff live or work at Dam Neck. Each year, over 17,000 students graduate from one of over 200 courses offered at this military training facility.[27]

Little Creek

The Navy began building the Amphibious Training Base at Little Creek in April 1942. Construction of the base was a concentrated effort. Five buildings a day were completed on a waterlogged bean field. The mud and adverse conditions allowed for drills focused on new methods and techniques, such as maneuvers perfecting the capture of enemy land comprised of difficult terrain.

The Amphibious Training Command, U.S. Atlantic Fleet, officially began operation on August 1, 1943. Functioning under the auspices of Little Creek were the Naval Frontier Base, Camp Bradford, and Camp Shelton. The Amphibious Training Command at Little Creek trained over 200,000 naval and 160,000 army and marine personnel in World War II. When the war ended, the command was deactivated, and the United States Naval Amphibious Base Little Creek was created. Congress allocated funds for developing and improving the facility in the early 1950s.[28]

The Naval Amphibious Base Little Creek is the largest base of its kind in the world. Serving as the major operation station for the amphibious forces of the United States Atlantic Fleet, it occupies over 2,100 acres of land in the northwest corner of Virginia Beach.[29] Over 15,000 military and civilian personnel work at the base, providing services to the twenty-seven home-ported ships and to seventy-eight additional residential commands or activities. [30]

In 1988, South Hampton Roads' first monument to all United States war veterans was built. The thirty-five foot structure is located on Pavilion Drive near the oceanfront. The memorial, costing $500,000, was six years in the making and was constructed from the design of three Virginia Beach students. On the dedication day, Congressman Owen Pickett stated that the Tidewater Veterans Memorial "will stand always as a solemn reminder of the high price of freedom and liberty."[31]

Courtesy of Virginia Beach Public Library

Tidewater Veterans Memorial, built 1988

Notes for Chapter 13

1. "Aircraft Attack Fails in Attempt to Sink Warship," *Norfolk Virginian-Pilot*, 21 July 1921, 1.
2. "Navy Acquires Princess Anne Landing Field," *Norfolk Virginian-Pilot*, 19 December 1940, 22.
3. "U.S. Acquires Creeds Land for Airfield," *Norfolk Virginian-Pilot*, 6 February 1941, 20.
4. "New Air Field, 441 Acres, for Navy at Pungo," *Norfolk Virginian-Pilot*, 21 March 1941, part 2, 14.
5. Marvin W. Schlegel, *Conscripted City: Norfolk in World War II* (Norfolk, Va.: Norfolk War History Commission, 1951), 31.
6. Ibid., 59.
7. Ibid., 361.
8. Ibid., 350.
9. Edward Rowe Snow, *Famous Lighthouses of America* (New York: Dodd, Mead & Company, 1955), 165-166.
10. Schlegel, 191.
11. Snow, 165-167.
12. "Map to Set Forth Need of Fortifications at Capes," *Virginian-Pilot*, 29 December 1909, 3.
13. Stephen S. Mansfield, *Princess Anne County and Virginia Beach: A Pictorial History* (Norfolk, Va.: The Donning Company/Publishers, 1989), 106.
14. James M. Jordan IV and Frederick Jordan, *Virginia Beach: A Pictorial History* (Richmond, Va.: Hale Publishing, 1974), 105.
15. "State Commission Receives Numerous Protests against Army Using Seashore Park," *Norfolk Virginian-Pilot*, 29 September 1940, part 2, 1.
16. "Fort Story Hospital Site is Relocated," *Norfolk Virginian-Pilot*, 5 October 1940, 16.
17. Schlegel, 20.
18. Rogers Dey Whichard, *The History of Lower Tidewater Virginia*, vol. 2 (New York: Lewis Historical Publishing, Inc., 1959), 119.
19. Jordan and Jordan, 14-15.
20. Dan Cragg, *Guide to Military Installations*, 4th ed. (Mechanicsburg, Pa.: Stackpole Books, 1994), 297.
21. Virginia Beach Department of Economic Development, "City of Virginia Beach 2001-2002 Data Sheet," from the website vbgov.com, http://www.vbgov.com/dept/econdev/ vgn_files/2001_english_datasheet.pdf, accessed on 11/06/2005.
22. Whichard, 103-104.
23. Patrick Evans-Hylton, *Hampton Roads: The World War II Years* (Charleston, SC: Arcadia Publishers, 2005), 53.
24. Jon W. Glass and Jack Dorsey, "Inside Oceana Naval Air Station," *Virginian-Pilot*, 25 July 2005, from the website PilotOnline.com, http://home.hamptonroads.com/stories/story.cfm? story=89691&ran=217337, accessed on 11/05/2005.
25. "Naval Air Station Oceana," from the website Wikipedia, http://en.wikipedia.org/wiki/ NAS_Oceana, accessed on 11/05/2005.
26. Whichard, 104.
27. "Dam Neck," from the website GlobalSecurity.org, www.globalsecurity.org/military/facility/dam-neck.htm, accessed on 11/06/2005.
28. Whichard, 102-103.
29. "Naval Amphibious Base Little Creek," from the website GlobalSecurity.org, www.globalsecurity.org/military/facility/little_creek.htm, accessed on 11/5/2005.
30. "Naval Amphibious Base Little Creek," from the website Wikipedia, http://en.wikipedia.org/ wiki/Little_Creek,_VA, accessed on 11/05/2005.
31. Lamar B. Graham, "Veterans Gather to Remember, Dedicate Memorial," *Virginian-Pilot*, 31 May 1988, D1, D3.

Chapter 14

The Merger

I n the 1950's, land in Princess Anne County adjacent to the city of Norfolk rapidly became suburbanized. Norfolk was extending city waterlines far out into the county to service the developing subdivisions. Princess Anne County and the City of Virginia Beach were dependent on Norfolk for their water supply. It was reasonable to assume that territorial claims eventually would follow the boundaries of Norfolk's waterlines.[1]

Traditionally, unincorporated county territory bordering an incorporated city was subject to municipal annexation. As county land adjacent to Norfolk became less rural and more urban in character, the city was allowed to annex such areas to accommodate urban growth. According to state laws, annexation claims were decided solely on the basis of orderly growth and development of the entire area, rather than the wishes of the residents. No provisions were made for a referendum by the city, county, or the area proposed for annexation.[2]

Annexation Problems

On January 1, 1959, Norfolk became the eighth largest city in the south by annexing 13 ½ square miles of Princess Anne County, which was home to 38,000 residents.[3] The politics of Princess Anne County and Virginia Beach were dominated by Sidney S. Kellam.

Kellam's family was prominent in both the political and civic affairs of the community. His father, Abel Kellam, was clerk of the circuit court of Princess Anne County for twenty years, and his brother, Floyd Kellam, was the circuit court judge. Sidney Kellam learned the techniques of politics firsthand, and in 1931 he was elected county treasurer. He ran for treasurer unopposed four more times, headed the Department of Conservation and Economic Development, and served eight years on Virginia's Democratic Committee. The Kellam organization was perhaps the strongest local political machine in Virginia. The organization was cohesive, well disciplined, and supported by the most influential segments of the community.[4]

The Kellam organization clearly recognized that Norfolk's annexations were likely to continue. To stop further annexation, the organization leaders lobbied unsuccessfully during Virginia's 1960 General Assembly to have the state's annexation law modified to protect Princess Anne County's territorial integrity.

Their lobbying prompted Norfolk to delay any further extension of water service into Princess Anne County. Water was a key factor in the growth of both the city and the county. Suburban tract developers were so enraged by the delay that Kellam appeared before the Norfolk City Council in April 1960 with a proposal for a five-year moratorium on annexation procedures against Princess Anne County. Kellam agreed not to lobby in the Virginia General Assembly for any changes in the state annexation laws. Also proposed was the appointment of a special joint committee to study the possibilities of "a metropolitan government" in Tidewater.[5] A seven-man committee was formed, with Kellam named as chairman.[6]

Considering Consolidation

Kellam's maneuvering had gained the county some needed time in diverting Norfolk's attention from annexation. Norfolk city officials were taken by surprise on October 3, 1961, when Virginia Beach and Princess Anne County publicly announced their intent to study merger possibilities.[7] In a newspaper advertisement on October 28, 1961, the Norfolk City Council stated their belief that "the proposed merger will not be helpful to the present progressive vitality of the Tidewater area or beneficial to the individual citizens of Princess Anne County or Virginia Beach."[8]

The threat of annexation by Norfolk was becoming very real for the county residents. Norfolk Mayor W.F. Duckworth hinted at possible repercussions to the residents of Princess Anne County. Duckworth stated if the city of Norfolk was prevented permanently from the normal, healthy expansion of most progressive cities, the citizens could be justifiably resentful.[9]

On December 5, 1961, the Norfolk City Council voted to cut off water service to areas of Princess Anne County if the voters ratified the merger. Although Mayor Duckworth and the city council refused to acknowledge the vote as a challenge, the county residents saw it as a threat. Earl W. Kingsbury, a representative of the Aragona

Civic League, raged, "They are squirting a water pistol at us. Let's merge."[10]

The Merger Campaign

The merger was a well-planned, well-executed political campaign, conducted by Sidney Kellam's Consolidation Study Committee. Members of the committee were R. Lee Bonney, Clayton Q. Nugent, R. L. Riggs, Frank E. Dickerson, A. L. Bonney, Alton Williams, Charges Burlage, J.W. Wood, D. L. Gregory, and N. C. Chandler. In October 1961 Kellam stated, "I'm confident that Princess Anne County is going to find some way to become a city." The key to the merger proposal was the county's desire to forestall any further annexations by Norfolk.[11]

By the end of October, the committee outlined consolidation problems, settled on the name of Virginia Beach, resolved joint political representation, and assessed the city and county indebtedness. The name "Virginia Beach" was approved because it

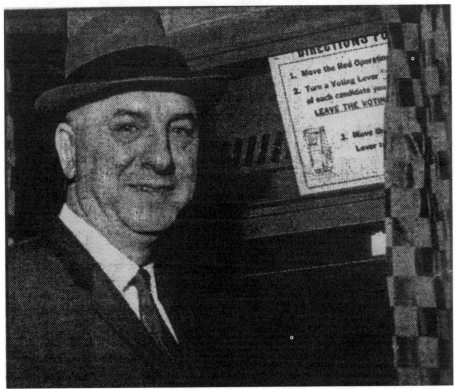

Courtesy of the *Virginian-Pilot* and the *Ledger-Star.* Supplement to the Virginia Beach *Beacon,* February 21, 1988

Sidney Kellam, voting in the 1962 referendum

was considered to be better known, particularly in business and tourist advertisements. The name "Princess Anne" was retained by renaming the Seaboard Magisterial District "the Princess Anne Borough." The principal seat of government was to be located at the Princess Anne Courthouse and became known as the Virginia Beach Municipal Center.

The respective elected officials decided the details for a city council-type representation among themselves. It appears that there were no consistent methods or criteria for deciding who would be the principal and/or the deputy officials in the consolidated city government structure. Thus, the county's board of supervisors and the city's councilmen all became members of the consolidated city council.[12]

The Richmond law firm of Hunton, William, Gay, Powell, and Gibson was retained to draw up a working charter and a consolidated agreement.[13] On November 4, the charter was presented to the public and endorsed by the Virginia Beach Chamber of Commerce. The Virginia Beach City Council and the Princess Anne Board of Supervisors unanimously approved the merger agreement and charter on November 10, 1961.[14]

The next step was to win acceptance at the polls on January 4, 1962. The referendum was the end result of a well organized political campaign carried to voters on a direct, personal, small group basis. Elected public officials were promoting the merger. Many of the people active in the initial phases of the proposed consolidation joined the campaign as members of the Speakers Bureau. They spoke to civic groups, women's clubs, church organizations, government classes, and even school assemblies. Public officials led rallies, were principal speakers, and served as "authorities" on the merger. Being familiar with local government and their specific offices, these officials were able to present in detail what effects the merger would have on the individual citizen.[15] Throughout November and December, virtually every organized group in Princess Anne County and Virginia Beach heard a presentation from a pro-merger speaker.[16]

Although little local opposition was voiced, several pointed questions were directed to the pro-merger leaders. In addition, a few letters to the editor appeared in the local newspaper. Opposition was strongest in the affluent areas near the resort city, such as Bay Colony, North Virginia Beach, and Birdneck Point. These residents had strong financial and emotional ties to Norfolk.[17]

In a final attempt to delay the referendum, Littleton B. Walker, a longtime Kellam foe, filed suit against the City of Virginia Beach and the County of Princess Anne, challenging the constitutionality of the merger. The case was not decided until April 17, 1962, several months after the referendum, when Walker's suit was dismissed and no appeal was made. Kellam had labeled the action "political propaganda filed under the guise of a legal suit." Kellam further accused Walker of "spending hundreds of dollars to run newspaper ads in an effort to confuse the people."[18]

The outcome at the polls never appeared to be in doubt. The voters overwhelmingly approved the merger. The official tabulation in Virginia Beach was 1,539 for and 242 against. In Princess Anne County the count was 7,476 for and 1,759 against.[19] The predominantly Black precinct of Seatack led all the polling places by a whopping 22-1 margin in favor the merger. Anti-merger forces did not carry a single precinct. The lowest margin of victory was Cape Henry precinct with a 3-2 margin.[20] The people had spoken. The merger campaign was over.

The City Charter and the General Assembly

After voter approval of the merger, the leadership focused on getting the merger charter passed by the General Assembly. V.A. Etheridge, treasurer of Virginia Beach, took up temporary residence in the Hotel Richmond to see the charter bill through this process.[21] Actually, Virginia Beach politicians had begun to lobby well in advance of the General Assembly session. During the preceding fall gubernatorial election, they had backed the state Democratic organization candidate and had produced organization majorities at the polls. Norfolk voters, on the other hand, failed to support the state organization candidates. As a result, in an "organization-dominated" 1962 General Assembly, there was little sympathy for Norfolk when Virginia Beach's charter bill came before the assembly.

For Virginia Beach it was simply a matter of collecting the rewards. The General Assembly handled the charter as a routine matter. They viewed the consolidation as being local in nature, an important factor in legislative thinking. They also accepted the "pro-mergerites" tenet that the merger would enhance, not stifle, future metropolitan cooperation.[22] The House of Delegates overwhelmingly approved the merger charter by a vote of 85 to 9.[23] It was approved and enacted by the General Assembly on February 28, 1962. The consolidation of the City of Virginia Beach and Princess Anne County would become effective on January 1, 1963.

The Transition

Once the charter was ratified, the transitional phase of the consolidation began. The transition lasted less than a year and went smoothly due to two factors. The first factor was that both Virginia Beach and Princess Anne County had a history of certain shared functions and officers. Shared functions included schools, health, welfare, library service, and mosquito control. The joint officers were the school superintendent, the clerk of the circuit court, and the commonwealth's attorney. The second factor was the dominance of the Kellam organization in both city and county affairs. The organization provided a unified political framework and approached transition as a group effort.

The existing Merger Executive Committee coordinated transition activities. This committee was headed by Ivan Mapp, the county commissioner of revenue, and included the county clerk of the circuit court, county treasurer, city treasurer, city commissioner of revenue, and city sergeant. The Merger Executive Committee met in joint sessions with the city council and the county board of supervisors.

Between March and November 1962, numerous special committees were appointed to study and to make recommendations on particular aspects of the consolidation. They included the Committee on Street Names and Numbers, the Committee on Equalization of Tax Assessments, the Water Committee, the Transportation Committee, the Committee to Study Garage Facilities, the Committee to Negotiate for the Purchase of Land, and the City Seal Committee.

In addition to the recommendations of these special committees, the Merger Executive Committee requested reports from city and county officials. These reports were compiled in order to identify problems and to define operational limits, functions, and responsibilities of the consolidated city departments.

By September 1962, most of the problems had been identified and attention turned to the actual setting up of the new city government. Numerous appointments were announced. Operational plans were finalized for the offices of commissioner of the revenue, treasurer, and high constable, and the city manager's salary was fixed. A legal publishing firm was engaged. Special taxes on amusements, food, lodging, and cigarettes were approved. Miscellaneous decisions on matters such as the slogan "World's Largest Resort City" were made.

The final joint session of the Merger Executive Committee and the two governing boards (one for the city, one for the county) took place on December 28, 1962. The City of Virginia Beach became a reality on January 1, 1963.[24]

The City of Virginia Beach

The charter of the consolidated city provided for a council/city manager form of government. Virginia Beach was divided into seven boroughs. The city which existed prior to the merger became the Virginia Beach Borough. The six remaining boroughs, Bayside, Blackwater, Kempsville, Lynnhaven, Princess Anne (formerly Seaboard), and Pungo, were the former six magisterial districts of Princess Anne County.

Eleven elected council members representing the seven boroughs comprised the city council. By a majority vote, the council selected one among them to be mayor and one to be vice-mayor. Since 1988 citizens have elected the mayor directly by popular vote.[25] The mayor presides over council meetings and acts as the ceremonial head of city government. The vice-mayor assumes the mayoral duties in the absence of the mayor. The city council appoints the city manager, who was the executive and administrative head of the city government. Hiring the city manager is based on executive and administrative qualifications.[26]

In its first formal meeting, held on January 1, 1963, the city council appointed the city manager, clerk, city attorney, welfare board, and police and fire trials board. The council also adopted twenty-seven city ordinances. At the meeting a mahogany plaque with a bronze copy of the official City Seal was presented to Mayor Frank A. Dusch.[27] The seal was designed by Mrs. H. Ashton Williamson, Jr. of Oak Grove. It bears the motto, "Landmarks of Our Nation's Beginning" and depicts the Cape Henry Lighthouse and the First Landing Cross on a sunlit beach. This scene is surrounded by an inner ring of strawberry leaves and an outer ring of leaping marlins.[28] A group of navy men aboard the USS *Amphion* made the bronze replica, and it was presented by Captain Joseph W. Crawford, Jr.[29]

The City of Virginia Beach continually grows in population and sophistication. In 1963 nearly 37 percent of the total acreage of the city was farm land, which outranked all the state's counties in yield per acre of corn and wheat.[30] However, the rural character that predominated in 1963 rapidly faded. The huge county farms gave way to subdivisions, office parks, shopping centers, and planned residential communities.

Notes for Chapter 14

1. Luther J. Carter, "Borough Offered by P.A.," *Virginian-Pilot*, 4 April 1960, 1, 5.
2. David G. Temple, *Merger Politics: Local Government Consolidation in Tidewater Virginia* (Charlottesville, Va.: University of Virginia Press, 1972), 17.
3. Gene Roberts, "Norfolk Becomes Eighth City in the South, Population-Wise," *Virginian-Pilot*, 1 January 1959, 36.
4. Temple, 39-41.
5. Ibid., 74.
6. "First Ripples of Metropolitan Study," *Virginian-Pilot*, 13 August 1960, 4.
7. "Merger Study Asked," *Virginian-Pilot*, 3 October 1961, 17.
8. George M. Kelley, "Norfolk Brands Merger as Progress Threat," *Virginian-Pilot*, 29 October 1962, 1.
9. Temple, 77.
10. Frank R. Blackford, " Beach-P.A. Merger Move Expected Monday," *Virginian-Pilot*, 4 November 1961, 1, 3.
11. William E. Tazwell, "Consolidation Study Committee Appointed," *Virginian-Pilot*, 5 October 1961, 31.
12. *Virginian-Pilot*, 4 November 1961, 1, 3.
13. Princess Anne –Virginia Beach Merger Committee Papers. Central Library Archives. Virginia Beach, Virginia.
14. *Virginian-Pilot*, 11 November 1961, 1.
15. Temple, 72.
16. Ibid., 80.
17. Frank R. Blackford, "Suburbia Shakes Old Norfolk Ties," *Virginian-Pilot*, 4 December 1961, 17.
18. Temple, 78-79.
19. Ibid., 82.
20. Frank R. Blackford, "Beach-P.A. Merger Wins by Sweeping 5-1 Margin," *Virginian-Pilot*, 5 January 1962, 1.
21. Temple, 99.
22. Ibid., 102-103.
23. George M. Kelley, "P.A.-Beach Charter Passes House, 85 to 9," *Virginian-Pilot*, 2 February 1962, 1.
24. Temple, 22-126.
25. Stephen S. Mansfield, *Princess Anne County and Virginia Beach: A Pictorial History* (Norfolk, Va.: The Donning Company/Publishers, 1989), 13.
26. "Charter for the City of Virginia Beach," *Virginian-Pilot*, 16 November 1961, 40.
27. Temple, 126.
28. Frank R. Blackford, "Housewife Designs New Beach Seal," *Virginian-Pilot*, 11 December 1962, 17.
29. Temple, 126.
30. Ibid., 137.

Chapter 15

Virginia Beach Today

A vital and thriving metropolis, the city of Virginia Beach has experienced growth in its population, business and industry, cultural and recreational opportunities, and services to citizens. New residents continually seek out Virginia Beach for all the amenities it offers, truly living up to its mission of being a "Community for a Lifetime."[1]

Population

Population growth in Virginia Beach has continued over the past forty years. The new city numbered 111,400 residents in 1963, the year Princess Anne County and Virginia Beach merged. The population mushroomed to 295,718 by 1983, a whopping increase of 165% over twenty years.[2] Current estimates place the population of the City of Virginia Beach at 432,092, with all indicators pointing to a continual steady growth in numbers of residents.[3]

Government and Quality of Life

The City of Virginia Beach is organized under the council/manager form of government. The city manager is appointed by the eleven-member elected city council and acts as chief executive officer. The mayor is elected by the citizens of Virginia Beach and serves a four-year term.[4] The city manager is responsible for implementing policies established by the council, while the mayor presides over council meetings and serves as spokesperson for the city. Meyera Oberndorf, the city's first directly elected mayor, was sworn into office on May 1, 1988. Mrs. Oberndorf has been reelected to the position in each subsequent city election.[5]

Quality of life in Virginia Beach is of paramount importance to city leaders, who consider safe neighborhoods a major priority. A recent survey shows that residents give city services an overall satisfaction rate of 92.6%. The number of citizens who agree that Virginia Beach is a safe place to live is even higher at 94.8%. Specific city services with a 95% or higher approval rating include police and fire department services, paramedic and rescue squad services, and the services offered by public libraries.[6] City leaders strive to maintain and even increase services to citizens, while exercising fiscal responsibility and insuring that city finances remain stable.[7]

The Lake Gaston Pipeline

For a number of years, a major challenge caused by the population boom in Virginia Beach was finding a dependable and economical source of drinking water. Numerous water supply alternatives were studied. The decision was made to build a pipeline to Lake Gaston, a reservoir located approximately 125 miles west of Virginia Beach.[8] A dozen years of discussion and contentious debate ensued. Finally, construction was completed on the Lake Gaston Pipeline in late 1997, and the water began flowing in January of 1998.[9] The Virginia Beach City Council approved a new licensing agreement with North Carolina and the other localities involved with the pipeline in May of 2003, insuring that city residents will have Lake Gaston to depend on as a reliable water source for the next 30 years.[10]

Education

With nearly 75,000 students, the Virginia Beach Public Schools is the second largest school system in Virginia, and among the 50 largest school divisions in the United States based on student enrollment. Currently, the school system numbers over 80 schools, including several secondary and post-secondary subject academies and specialty centers.[11]

One such specialty educational facility is the Advanced Technology Center, the result of a partnership between Tidewater Community College, the Virginia Beach City Public Schools, and the City of Virginia Beach. The 137,000 square foot facility which opened in 2002 prepares students for careers or college studies in information technology, telecommunications, and computerized manufacturing and engineering.[12]

Many opportunities for higher education are available to students in Virginia Beach. Tidewater Community College and Regent University are located in the city, and large satellite campuses of Virginia Tech, the University of Virginia, Norfolk State University, and Old Dominion University provide four-year degrees locally.[13] Adding to the educational opportunities in the area is the Virginia Beach Higher Education Center. Run by Old Dominion University and Norfolk State University, this unique facility was designed to support an array of graduate and undergraduate programs that meet the higher education needs of the community.[14]

Education opportunities of all kinds are available from the Virginia Beach Public Library. The Virginia Beach Public Library provides the materials, services, programming, and technology needed to foster the literate populace that is essential to democracy. The twelve library facilities and information agencies of the Virginia Beach Public Library offer learning opportunities to all citizens of the community and serve as a vital resource in the pursuit of lifelong learning.[15]

Industry and Economy

The economic base of the City of Virginia Beach is highly diversified. Sectors of the local economy include agriculture, business and industry, construction and real estate, conventions, retail and wholesale trade, and tourism. Real estate assessments for properties in the city continue to rise, but city officials attempt to keep taxes affordable for residents by reducing real estate tax rates whenever feasible.[16] The city also boasts a higher median family income than the region's average.[17]

Agriculture remains a vital economic element in Virginia Beach. Acres under cultivation numbered over 27,000 in 2005, resulting in an economic impact of over $80 million.[18] Estimates indicate that nearly 3 million out-of-town visitors arrived in Virginia Beach in 2004. These visitors spent $785 million in Virginia Beach and created more than 10,000 jobs in the city. Direct city revenues from tourism generated over $67 million. When visitors spend money in Virginia Beach, other localities in the region benefit. Research reveals that an additional 5,169 jobs and $389 million in expenditures are created in the region due to tourism in the City of Virginia Beach.[19]

The opening of the Virginia Beach Convention Center will cause a significant impact on convention business in the city. Built on the site of the Pavilion, the previous convention hall which opened in 1980, the Virginia Beach Convention Center includes 150,000 square feet of exhibit space, 55,000 square feet of meeting and ballroom space, and 2,600 parking spaces on site. It is estimated that one national or international convention of 5,000 delegates will generate over $4.5 million in direct sales and over $227,000 in direct taxes to the city.[20]

Courtesy of Carole J. Oste, Public Information Office, City of Virginia Beach

Strawberry Fields

Also contributing to the increased economic vitality is the Town Center of Virginia Beach. Its signature building, the Armada Hoffler Tower, is a landmark visible throughout Hampton Roads and is the second tallest building in Virginia. At the core of the Central Business District in the Pembroke area of Virginia Beach, the Town Center spans over 17 city blocks. It provides a mix of upscale retail establishments, luxury residences, office areas, restaurants, and a business class hotel. At full capacity, the Town Center will have a living and working population of over 24,000.[21]

The Military

Virginia Beach is home to four military bases which greatly affect the economy of the city and the region. Located in the southern part of the city, Naval Air Station Oceana is the largest master jet base in the United States. Nearby is Dam Neck, a training base for combat direction and control systems. Little Creek Naval Amphibious Base is positioned in the western part of the city bordering Norfolk, while the U.S. Army facility Fort Story is found in the north end of Virginia Beach where the Atlantic Ocean meets the Chesapeake Bay.[22]

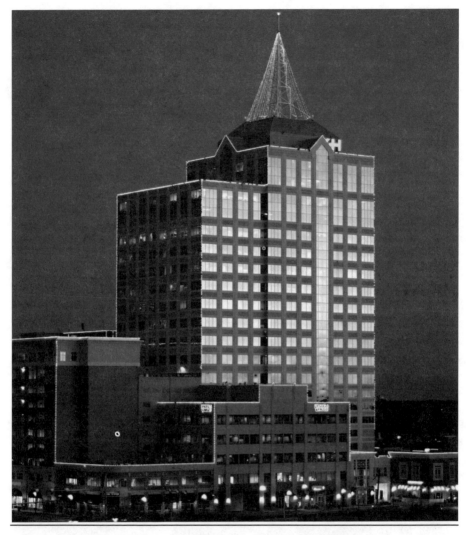

Courtesy of Carole J. Oste, Public Information Office, City of Virginia Beach

Armada Hoffler Tower in Town Center, Virginia Beach

After surviving the threat of base closures in the mid-1990s, the City of Virginia Beach was sent reeling by another ruling of the Defense Base Realignment and Closure (BRAC) Commission in 2005. Citing concerns about encroachment and development near NAS Oceana, the BRAC Commission required the city and state to enact ordinances to quell encroachment and fund the roll back of development in NAS Oceana's highest accident potential zone by March of 2006, or face closure of the base.

In August 2005, the city and state announced a series of initiatives intended to show the BRAC Commission a commitment to limiting development pressure around NAS Oceana. The city created work groups to analyze the land use and economic impact of the realignment of NAS Oceana. Legal issues and options were examined, and methods to keep the public informed were developed.[23] The city-state plan for compliance was submitted March 31, 2006, with the BRAC Commission's ruling expected in June 2006.[24] Whatever the final decision, the City of Virginia Beach will maintain close ties to the military community and continue to thrive.

Recreation and Cultural Opportunities

Virginia Beach has excellent natural resources and climate. The natural lands and waterways surrounding Virginia Beach are among some of the most pristine and undiscovered ecological areas along the mid-Atlantic.[25] A challenge presented by the city's growing population is maintaining the area's natural environment.[26]

Residents and visitors to Virginia Beach can enjoy the outdoors at numerous locations. First Landing State Park measures over 2,800 acres of wetlands and 1.25 miles of beachfront. Known for its dunes, wetlands, and trails off the Chesapeake Bay, First Landing State Park offers swimming, boating, hiking, and camping.[27] Located

Photo by Carole J. Oste, Public Information Office, City of Virginia Beach

Virginia Beach Scenic Waterway System
When formally opened in September 1986, it became the first locally developed comprehensive water trail system in the Commonwealth of Virginia. Visitors and residents can enjoy a variety of recreational activities on these scenic waterways.

in the southern part of Virginia Beach is False Cape State Park, a 4,300 acre spread with 5.9 miles of beachfront. Hiking, biking, and boating can be enjoyed by visitors to the park, where an unspoiled and protected ecological environment is maintained.[28] Bordering False Cape State Park is the Back Bay National Wildlife Refuge. Containing over 8,000 acres, the Back Bay Wildlife Refuge is situated on and around a thin strip of coastline typical of barrier islands found along the Atlantic and Gulf coasts. Habitats include beaches, dunes, woodlands, farm fields, and marshes. The majority of the marshlands in the refuge are on islands located within the waters of Back Bay.[29]

The City of Virginia Beach Department of Parks and Recreation oversees 208 municipal parks encompassing 4,000 acres. These include neighborhood, community, and district parks and other open spaces. Each park is unique and offers something for everyone, from playgrounds and ball fields to picnic shelters and tennis courts.[30] The city also operates three municipal golf courses which complement the fourteen additional private, public, and military courses located in Virginia Beach.[32] The city runs six community recreation centers. Each recreation center has an indoor swimming pool, indoor gymnasium, and ample room and meeting space for a variety of programs.[33]

Of world renown is one particular city park, Mount Trashmore on Edwin Drive. Spanning 165 acres and featuring a sixty foot high, 800 foot long "mountain," Mount Trashmore was built by compacting layers of solid waste and clean soil.[34] With the help of federal and state funds, construction began in the early 1970s using 640,000 tons of garbage. This project demonstrated a viable, ecologically safe alternative to burying or burning sold waste.[35] Mount Trashmore officially opened as a city park on October 5, 1974.[36]

Three of the city's parks are located on the Boardwalk at the oceanfront, offering staged entertainment as well as a place for people to congregate, stroll, or stop and enjoy the ocean view. The newest oceanfront park on 31st Street and Atlantic Avenue is aptly named Neptune Park. Home to the stunning twelve ton bronze statue of King Neptune crafted by Virginia sculptor Paul DiPasquale, Neptune Park is bounded on its south side by the new luxury Hilton Hotel. The 17th and 24th Street parks are also favorite destinations for oceanfront visitors seeking live entertainment or a place to gather.[37]

The City of the Virginia Beach offers many cultural facilities and arenas. The Virginia Beach Amphitheater opened in the spring of 1996, bringing large concert productions by world-famous performing artists to the city. Built on a ninety-six acre field behind Princess

Courtesy of Carole J. Oste, Public Information Office, City of Virginia Beach

Virginia Beach Amphitheater, opened 1996

Anne Park,[38] the amphitheater has 7,500 reserved theater-style seats under the pavilion roof and 12,500 festival lawn seating spots on the grassy hill behind it. There are five giant video screens and a state-of-the-art sound system to guarantee unobstructed viewing and top-notch sound.[39]

The Virginia Beach Sportsplex which opening in 1998, is the first facility in the United States specifically designed and constructed for professional soccer. The three-level stadium is occasionally used for other field sports and has a seating capacity of up to 10,000.[40] It is currently the home of the Virginia Beach Mariners Professional Soccer Team.[41]

A welcome addition to the cultural venues in the City of Virginia Beach will be the Sandler Center for the Performing Arts. Due to open in 2007, this arena will be the city's cultural centerpiece: a professional-quality facility celebrating the arts and showcasing the wealth of our region's cultural resources. Located in the heart of The Town Center, the Sandler Center will have a 1,200 seat performance hall and an outdoor performance plaza.[42]

Courtesy of Carole J. Oste, Public Information Office, City of Virginia Beach

Virginia Aquarium and Marine Science Center

The Virginia Aquarium and Marine Science Center has been a vital part of the Virginia Beach community for decades. Voted one of the top ten marine science aquarium museums in the United States,[43] the Virginia Aquarium has 800,000 gallons of aquariums and over 300 hands-on exhibits and live animal habitats. The 120,000 square foot facility hosts 650,000 visitors annually, including more than 100,000 school children.[44]

Residents and tourists alike enjoy the Contemporary Arts Center of Virginia. This nonprofit museum and art education facility fosters awareness, exploration and understanding of the significant art of our time. The Center offers changing exhibitions of paintings, sculpture, photography, glass, video, and other visual media from internationally, nationally, and regionally acclaimed artists.[45]

One of several noteworthy maritime sites in Virginia Beach is the Old Coast Guard Station. Housed in a lifesaving station dating back to 1903, the Old Coast Guard Station has maritime, lifesaving, and shipwreck exhibits on two floors.[46] On 25th Street, a block up the Boardwalk from the Old Coast Guard Station, is the Norwegian Lady. A gift to the people of Virginia Beach from the people of Moss, Norway, the statue commemorates the tragic wreck of the Norwegian ship *Dictator* off the shores of Virginia Beach in 1891.[47]

Diversity

As a result of population growth in Virginia Beach, the city has seen a sizable increase in ethnic diversity. The City of Virginia Beach values this variety and has made promoting and fostering racial, ethnic, and cultural understanding an official part of the city's strategic plan to create a Community for a Lifetime.[48]

Courtesy of Amy Belcher, Virginia Beach Public Libraries

King Neptune, sculpture by Paul DiPasquale

The ethnicity of the citizens in Virginia Beach is evident from recent Census population estimates. In 2004, Hispanic and Latino residents numbered nearly 20,500. Census estimates for the same year indicated an Asian population in the city of approximately 25,400, with Filipino citizens comprising 17,700 of that number. An estimated 86,350 African Americans resided in Virginia Beach in 2004.[49]

The Virginia Beach Human Rights Commission was established to promote cultural understanding and advocate for the human rights of the diverse citizenry of Virginia Beach. Functioning under the auspices of the City of Virginia Beach Department of Human Resources, the HRC's mission is to institute, conduct, and engage in educational and informational programs to further a mutual understanding and respect among citizens of the city. Serving as a forum for discussion of human rights issues and providing assistance to persons who believe their rights have been violated are also goals of the Virginia Beach Human Rights Commission.[50]

Another way the city has responded to the growing multiculturalism in Virginia Beach is the establishment of the International Language Collection in the city's public libraries. The Virginia Beach Public Library provides materials in Tagalog and Spanish to meet the needs of Filipino and Hispanic residents. Along

Courtesy of City of Virginia Beach

Virginia Beach Resort

with Tagalog and Spanish, the public libraries carry items in seven additional languages, which are part of the curriculum of the Virginia Beach Public Schools.[51]

History has proven that Virginia Beach is an innovative and resourceful city, dedicated to maintaining an excellent quality of life for its citizens. The input of citizens is a key to planning for the future, while honoring the past. As Mayor Meyera Oberndorf says, "Just as Virginia Beach is working to build a successful city for today and tomorrow, we are working to preserve what is important in our past. Community input is the lifeline of strong government. And when we collaborate, we can achieve greatness."[52]

From the beginning, Princess Anne County and Virginia Beach have experienced growth, development, and numerous challenges. There will be much planning for years to come. The history of Virginia Beach does not end here, and will be for future generations to create. The sands of time will continue to shape *The Beach*.

Notes for Chapter 15

1. *Community for a Lifetime: A Strategy to Achieve City Council's Vision for the Future*, 2nd ed. (Virginia Beach, Va.: City of Virginia Beach Printing Office).

2. Paul Harris, Management Services, City of Virginia Beach, interview by staff of the Virginia Beach Public Library, 1 May 2006.

3. United States Census, "Virginia Beach, Virginia, General Demographic Characteristics: 2004".

4. "About Our City – Government," from the website http://www.vbgov.com/about/0,1111,1883,00.html, accessed on 05/01/2006.

5. Michael Jon Khandelwal, "Take Me To Your Leader: Mayor Meyera Oberndorf shepherds the city of Virginia Beach," from the website http://www.hamptonroadsmagazine.com/issues/0505/leader.php, accessed on 05/01/2006.

6. Jeannine Perry, Senior Project Manager, Continental Research Associates, Inc., Norfolk, Virginia, interview by staff of the Virginia Beach Public Library, 1 May 2006.

7. *Community for a Lifetime: A Strategy to Achieve City Council's Vision for the Future*, 2nd ed. (Virginia Beach, Va.: City of Virginia Beach Printing Office).

8. Thomas Leahy, Water Resources Engineer for Virginia Beach Department of Public Utilities, interview by staff of the Virginia Beach Public Library, Virginia Beach, Virginia, July 1996.

9. "The Year in Review Beach Greets Water," *Virginian-Pilot*, 4 July 1998, from NewsBank database America's Newspapers, accessed on 05/02/2006.

10. "Beach Approves New Agreement to Use Lake Gaston," *Virginian-Pilot*, 28 May 2003, from NewsBank database America's Newspapers, accessed on 05/02/2006.

11. "School Guide – School Year 2005-2006: An Overview of Virginia Beach City Public Schools," from the website http://www.vbschools.com/curriculum/guides/school/school_overview.asp, accessed on 05/02/2006.

12. "Beach-TCC Tech Center Nears Completion – After Months of Delay, Building is Scheduled to Open to Classes by October's End," *Virginian-Pilot*, 15 October 2002, from Newsbank database America's Newspapers, accessed on 05/02/2006.

13. "Education and Demographics," from the website http://www.vbgov.com/dept/econdev/education_demographics/0,1854,11249,00.html, accessed on 05/02/2006.

14. "Virginia Beach Higher Education Center," from the website http://www.odu.edu/ao/vbhec/, accessed on 05/02/2006.

15. "Library Mission, Vision and Strategic Plan," from the website http://www.vbgov.com/dept/library/aboutus/0,1511,17598,00.html, accessed on 05/02/2006.

16. "Cities Propose Tax Rate Cuts," *Virginian-Pilot*, 29 March 2006, from Newsbank database America's Newspapers, accessed on 05/04/2006.

17. "About Our City – Government," from the website http://www.vbgov.com/about/0,1111,1883,00.html, accessed on 05/01/2006.

18. Calvin A. Schiemann, Virginia Cooperative Extension, Virginia Beach, Virginia, interview by staff of the Virginia Beach Public Library, 3 May 2006.

19. City of Virginia Beach Convention and Visitor Center, *Economic Impact Statement*, from the website http://www.vbgov.com/dept/cvd/vgn_files/04ecimpct.pdf, accessed on 05/03/2006.

20. "Virginia Beach Convention Center – General Overview," from the website http://www.vbgov.com/dept/cvd/vbcc/0,1826,8364,00.html, accessed on 05/04/2006.

21. "About the Town Center of Virginia Beach," from the website http://www.vabeachtowncenter.com/Town_Center_of_Virginia_Beach.php, accessed on 05/01/2006.

22. "Virginia Beach, Virginia – Military Bases," from the website http://en.wikipedia.org/wiki/Virginia_Beach, accessed on 05/04/2006.

23. "BRAC – Frequently Asked Questions," from the website http://www.vbgov.com/dept/brac/0,2130,21877,00.html, accessed on 05/04/2006.

24. "Naval Station's Fate Comes Down to One Sentence – All 238 Words of It," *Virginian-Pilot*, 11 April 2006, from NewsBank database America's Newspapers, accessed on 05/04/2006.

25. C. Oral Lambert, Jr., Chief of Staff for the City of Virginia Beach, interview by staff of the Virginia Beach Public Library, questionnaire, Virginia Beach, Virginia, 29 September 1995, 1.

26. "Virginia Beach," from the website http://www.mobiltravelguide.com, accessed on 05/05/2006.

27. "Virginia Department of Conservation & Recreation – First Landing State Park," from the website http://www.dcr.state.va.us/parks/1stland.htm, accessed on 05/05/2006.

28. "Virginia Department of Conservation & Recreation – False Cape State Park," from the website http://www.dcr.virginia.gov/parks/falscape.htm, accessed on 05/05/2006.

29. "United States Fish and Wildlife Service – Back Bay National Wildlife Refuge," from the website http://www.fws.gov/backbay/, accessed on 05/05/2006.

30. "Parks & Recreation - Park Facilities," from the website http://www.vbgov.com/dept/parks/parks/, accessed on 05/05/2006.

31. "Parks & Recreation - Golf Courses," from the website http://www.vbgov.com/dept/parks/golf/, accessed on 05/05/2006.

32. *National Golf Foundation Golf Course Directory 2005*, "Virginia Beach, Virginia," (Jupiter, Fl.: National Golf Foundation of Jupiter, Florida, 2005), 1749-1751.

33. "Parks & Recreation Centers," from the website http://www.vbgov.com/dept/parks/centers/, accessed on 05/05/2006.

34. "Mount Trashmore Park," from the website http://www.vbgov.com/e-gov/vbcsg/faqinfo/0,1172,6128,00.html, accessed on 05/05/2006.

35. Ruby Jean Phillips, "Mountain of Trash," *Virginia Beach Beacon Visitors Guide*, 29 July 1973, n.p.

36. Jim Stiff, "Trashmore Municipal Park Opens Oct. 5," *The Beacon*, 4 October 1974, 21.

37. "King Neptune: Rising from the Sea," from the website http://sunnydayguide.com/virginiabeach/features/neptunepark.hmtl, accessed on 05/04/2006.

38. "Music in the Air – An $18.5 Million Dream Has Materialized in the Fields Near Princess Anne Park," *Virginian-Pilot*, 15 May 1996, from Newsbank database America's Newspapers, accessed on 12/16/2005.

39. "Verizon Wireless Virginia Beach Amphitheater," from the website http://home.hamptonroads.com/funplaces/detail.cfm?placeID=1219, accessed on 05/05/2006.

40. "Parks and Rec Takes Over Sportsplex Operations," *Virginian-Pilot*, 9 February 2003, from Newsbank database America's Newspapers, accessed on 12/14/2005.

41. "Discover the Sportsplex Amenities," from the website http://www.vbgov.com/common/printable/0,1359,1682,00.html, accessed on 12/14/2005.

42. "The Sandler Center for Performing Arts at Virginia Beach," from the website http://www.vbgov.com/dept/arts/sandlercenter/, accessed on 04/05/2006.

43. "Virginia Beach," from the website http://www.mobiltravelguide.com, accessed on 05/05/2006.

44. "Virginia Marine Science Museum – What is the Annual Attendance of the Virginia Science Museum," from the website http://www.vmsm.com/faq.html, accessed on 05/05/2006.

45. "Contemporary Art Center: General Information," from the website http://www.cacv.org/generalInfo/index.asp, accessed on 05/05/2006.

46. "The Old Coast Guard Station," from the website http://www.oldcoastguardstation.com/collectioncontent.htm, accessed on 05/05/2006.

47. "Virginia Beach – What to See and Do" from the website http://www.mobiltravelguide.com, accessed on 05/05/2006.

48. *Community for a Lifetime: A Strategy to Achieve City Council's Vision for the Future*, 2nd ed. (Virginia Beach, Va.: City of Virginia Beach Printing Office).

49. United States Census, "Virginia Beach, Virginia, General Demographic Characteristics: 2004".

50. "Resident Advocacy," from the website http://www.vbgov.com/dept/hr/residents/0,1781,11298,00.html, accessed on 05/04/2006.

51. Virginia Beach Department of Public Libraries, *Foreign Language Materials Report*, (Virginia Beach, Va.: Department of Public Libraries, 2002), 3.

52. Mayor Meyera Oberndorf, "State of the City Address," *Virginian-Pilot*, 26 March 2006, from Newsbank database America's Newspapers, accessed on 05/01/2006.

Appendix I

A Survey of Historic Families

In addition to the historic families discussed in Chapter 3, others became important to Princess Anne County and the City of Virginia Beach. They include:

CORNICK/CORNIX

Simon Cornick (Simond Cornix) received a certificate for 650 acres in 1653 for transporting thirteen persons to Virginia. Four of the thirteen were Jane, assumed to be his wife, and three children, Martha, William, and Thomas. The acreage was apparently not awarded until 1657, when William Cornick acquired the patent for the acreage due his father, Simon. The property was located south of Virginia Beach Boulevard in an area known as Salisbury Plains. This area is now included in the property of NAS Oceana.[1]

William Cornick's wife, Elizabeth, was the daughter of John Martin and the sister of Adam Keeling's wife, Anne. William and Elizabeth's children were Joel (who inherited Salisbury Plains and married Elizabeth, the daughter of Henry Woodhouse), Elizabeth (the wife of Thomas Cannon), Barbara (who married Captain Francis Morse), and Martin, John, William, and Simon.[2]

KEELING

Thomas Keeling came to Virginia as one of the 105 headrights of Adam Thorowgood's 1635 patent. In that same year, Keeling acquired 100 acres of land on Back River. He served as a vestryman of Lynnhaven Parish in 1640. Upon his death he left six children. His eldest son, Adam (godson of Adam Thorowgood), married Anne Martin (sister of William Cornick's wife, Elizabeth). The Keelings, like the Woodhouses and Cornicks, were large landowners in the area south of London Bridge and Oceana.[3] *See Appendix II for information on the Keeling House.*

LAMBERT

In 1635, Ensign Thomas Lambert patented the point of land on the Elizabeth River which still bears his name. By 1648, Captain Lambert received a grant for a tract in Lynnhaven Parish called Puggett's Neck on Little Creek. In 1652, he was a Burgess for Lower Norfolk County. He died in 1671, leaving his estate to his four daughters. In the same year, his four sons-in-law, George Fowler, Henry Snaile, Richard Drout, and John Weblin, filed a deed of partition for the Puggett's Neck property as co-heirs. As his wife's share, John Weblin received a tract of land that included the residence now known as the Weblin House.[4]

LAND

Francis Land (I) settled in Lower Norfolk County (later Princess Anne County) and had patented over 1,000 acres of land by the time of his death in the mid-1650s. Six generations of the Land family (all six heads of the household were named Francis) operated the plantation on a large tract of land, general location of which is known although exact boundaries are not.[5]

The Land family raised tobacco as their cash crop during the first two generations. The 1760 inventory of Francis Thorowgood Land indicates that they had changed to wheat and oats by the mid-eighteenth century. In addition, the Land family raised cattle, hogs, and sheep. An extensive vegetable garden probably helped to make the plantation self-sufficient.[6] The Land family members were active as church and government leaders. *For information on the Francis Land House see Chapter 3.*

LAWSON

The Lawson family came to Virginia via Bermuda. Captain Thomas Lawson and his wife, Margaret Bray, had been shipwrecked in 1609 while aboard the *Seaventure*. Their son, Anthony, was born soon after their arrival at Jamestown. Anthony had two sons, George and Anthony (II). Educated in England, Anthony (II) returned to Virginia from Ireland in 1668 and settled on the Eastern Branch of the Elizabeth River, adjoining the William Moseley and William Hancock properties.

Beginning with his first patent in 1673, Anthony (II) amassed extensive land holdings. He was, together with Captain William

Robinson, one of the investors in Norfolk Town lots in 1680. Anthony (II) married Mary Gookin Moseley, daughter of Sarah Offley Thorowgood Gookin Yeardley and the widow of William Moseley (II) and Edward Moseley (II).[7] The fifty-one acres for the town were situated on the north side of the Eastern Branch of the Elizabeth River on property purchased from Simon Handcock (Hancock).[8]

MOSELEY

William Moseley, his wife, Susannah, and their sons, William (II) and Arthur, were in Lower Norfolk County probably as early as 1649. In 1650, William (I) received a certificate for 150 acres due him for the transportation of eleven persons to Virginia. In 1652, he was granted a patent for land in Lynnhaven Parish. His manor, Rolleston, was located on the west side of the first creek east of Broad Creek and on the north side of the Eastern Branch of the Elizabeth River. Moseley became prominent in the county and served as a justice of its court. He died in 1655.

A deed William Moseley made to Colonel Francis Yeardley in 1652 and an earlier (1650) letter of his wife's addressed to Colonel Yeardley tell of the dire circumstances of the Moseleys upon their arrival in Virginia. Their lack of ready cash made it necessary to sell the family jewels for livestock. Colonel Francis Yeardley and his wife, Sarah Offley Thorowgood Gookin Yeardley, received one gold hat band, one gold and enamel buckle set with diamonds, one enameled jewel set with diamonds, and one enameled gold ring set with one diamond, one ruby, one "Sapphyr," and one emerald. In return for these pieces, Colonel Yeardley gave the Moseleys two oxen, two steers, and five cows.[9]

William (I) and Susannah's son, Captain William Moseley (II), was a justice in 1662. He married Mary Gookin, daughter of Sarah Offley Thorowgood Gookin Yeardley and John Gookin. Arthur Moseley, William (I) and Susannah's other son, married Simon Hancock's (Handcock) daughter. Arthur became one of the earliest lot owners in Norfolk.[10] Generations of Moseleys represented Princess Anne as justices, burgesses, and vestrymembers.

MURRAY

David Murray settled on the south side of the Eastern Branch of the Elizabeth River about 1650. He received a grant of 300 acres.[11] Richard Murray, a great-grandson, operated a commercial flax business on the property. It was conveniently located for the local shipping industry and may have provided the flax used in ropes and sails. There were outbuildings for the business, including a flax-drying shed. Early deeds refer to a flax pond on the Murray property. Richard built gambrel-roofed brick houses for his three sons near the present intersection of Indian River Road and Military Highway.[12]

SAUNDERS

Jonathan Saunders arrived in Princess Anne County in 1695 to be rector of Lynnhaven Parish. He married Mary Bennett Ewell, the widow of Thomas Ewell. Jonathan and Mary had two children, John and Mary. Following Jonathan's death, Mary Bennett Ewell Saunders married Maximillian Boush, a wealthy Norfolk merchant. Together they had twelve additional children.

John's son, Jonathan, built Pembroke Manor in 1764. He raised cattle, sheep, and hogs.[13] Jonathan's son, John, inherited the manor in 1775. That same year, he followed the lead of his guardian and brother-in-law, Jacob Ellegood, and answered Lord Dunmore's call to arms. He returned to Princess Anne in 1780 as a member of the British Army to head the forces at Kemp's (or Kempe's) Landing.[14]

Following the end of the American Revolution, John Saunders requested restitution by the British government for possessions he had lost in Virginia. These included "eight hundred acres of very good land with a large and valuable new brick dwelling house, an overseer's house, two kitchens, a barn and other out-houses, two apple orchards of more seven hundred bearing trees...." Also included were furniture, books, crops, sheep, and twelve slaves who were listed by name.[15] Following the American Revolution, John Saunders studied law in London, moved to New Brunswick, Canada, became First Justice of the Province, and fulfilled the potential he had shown as a young man in Princess Anne County.[16]

WALKE

Thomas Walke arrived in Princess Anne County from Barbados in 1662. He brought with him money and furniture. His household goods included eighteen Russian leather chairs, a Spanish olivewood chest, a silver-headed cane, and two "silver hilted pistols."[17] He remained a bachelor until 1689, when he married Mary, the daughter of Anthony Lawson. Their three children were Anthony, Thomas, and Mary. When Thomas Walke (I) died in 1694/5,[18] the inventory of his estate listed large amounts of Spanish and other foreign coin.[19] In a country where tobacco and tobacco warehouse receipts were used universally as money, the existence of coin was extremely unusual. In 1697, his executors purchased the land, which was to become Anthony Walke's manor of Fairfield.[20] Generations of Walke descendants left a long history of activity in church and government affairs.

WISHART/LOVETT/KEMP(E)

In 1673, James Wishart purchased property from William Richerson, who had previously acquired it from Adam Thorowgood (II). When James Wishart died in 1679/80, he left his plantation in Little Creek to his son William. Another son, James, inherited the property on which he, James, was residing. Two additional sons, Thomas and John, and two daughters, Joyce and Frances, were also mentioned in his will.[21] Thomas Wishard (Wishart), the youngest son of James (I), married Mary, daughter of James Kemp. James Kemp had married Ann, the widow of Lancaster Lovett (a church warden in Lynnhaven in 1650 and first of four generations of Lancaster Lovetts). The Kemp family established itself at the head of the Eastern Branch of the Elizabeth River, which soon became known as Kempe's (or Kemp's) Landing, now called Kempsville.[22]

Notes for Appendix I

1. Sadie Scott Kellam and V. Hope Kellam, *Old Houses in Princess Anne Virginia* (Portsmouth, Va.: Printcraft, 1931), 105-106.
2. Ibid., 106-107.
3. Rogers Dey Whichard, *The History of Lower Tidewater Virginia,* vol. 1 (New York: Lewis Historical Publishing Company, Inc., 1959), 277-278.
4. Whichard, vol. 1, 279.
5. n.a., untitled, from the Francis Land House, (typescript, rev. 7/90), unpaged.
6. Ibid., unpaged.
7. Whichard, vol. 1, 279.
8. Florence Kimberly Turner, *Gateway to the New World: A History of Princess Anne County, Virginia 1607-1824* (Easley, S.C.: Southern Historical Press, 1984), 109.
9. Whichard, vol. 1, 275.
10. Ibid., 275.
11. Turner, 116.
12. Louisa Venable Kyle, "Flax-Drying House Built in 1738 Is Reminder of Earliest Industry." 20 July 1952, part 5, 3.
13. Turner, 189.
14. Ibid., 192.
15. Ibid., 195-196.
16. Ibid., 197.
17. Ibid., 134.
18. Kellam and Kellam, 174-175.
19. Turner, 134.
20. Whichard, vol. 1, 278.
21. Kellam and Kellam, 50.
22. Ibid., 205-206.

Appendix II

A Survey of Historic Homes

Because the City of Virginia Beach grew from rural rather than urban roots, the historic houses which remain are tucked away among modern subdivisions and spread across the landscape of the city. There is no concentrated area, such as an historic district, with an accumulation of sites to be preserved. To insure preservation, each house must stand on its own merits and find its own supporters. The Inventory of Historic Buildings and Sites by Age and Locations: As of July 1, 1989, *categorizes buildings and sites dating from the seventeenth through twentieth centuries. At the time of its publication, there were 320 historic buildings in the city. The following is a short list of some of these interesting properties.*

BAYVILLE FARMS
4137 First Court Road

This 1822 house was built by Peter Singleton (II) on property that was in the original Adam Thorowgood land grant. He inherited the land through his mother Sukio[1] (Suzanna or Sukey)[2] Thorowgood. Peter Singleton (II) was a gambler and lost the house and land. James Garrison, the next owner, built a race track on the property and raised Arabian horses. One of them, Wagner, was so successful in local races that, in 1839, Garrison sent him to New Orleans and to Kentucky to race. He beat every horse he raced against, including the more renowned Grey Eagle.[3]

Additions to the house include two porches and a guest house built on the foundation of the old kitchen. The guest house chimney is built with bricks from the kitchen.[4] A 1936 book gives this twentieth-century view of the property:

> *Standing on the lawn at "Bayville Manor" a beautiful picture is presented. Rows of peonies, azaleas, tulip . . . bulbs and shrubs grow in profusion . . . thousands of vari-colored blooms – more than 1000 peonies . . . blend perfectly.*[5]

The tradition of raising prize livestock continued into the second half of the twentieth century. In 1964, the dairy at Bayville Farms won the Premier Breeder Trophy and awards for the best females in the Guernsey class of the National Dairy Congress.[6]

Part of the farm was sold in 1990 to developers who built Church Point on First Court Road. The farm, which had at one time included the entire peninsula bounded by Shore Drive and First Court Road, was converted to a golf course. The houses on the property were retained by the Burroughs, Tyler, and Stanton families.[7] Bayville Farm is on the National Register of Historic Places.

BELL HOUSE
805 Oceana Boulevard

The only house of its type remaining in Virginia Beach, the Bell House is believed to have been built by Joshua James (II) about 1820. The house is typical of those built in the early part of the nineteenth century.[8] Joshua James (II) married Mary Dale Woodhouse in 1817. He wed Maria Capps in 1847, after the death of his first wife. Joshua James (II) died in 1860. Maria later married Alexander W. Bell, whose name the house retains.

The house continued to change hands, owned by William Cooke, the Whitehursts, the Parkers, and others. In 1937, it was purchased by Charlie Cartwright who had the house wired for electricity. In 1942, A. T. Taylor bought the Bell House.[9] He restored the house and added to the property until it was about 1,000 acres.[10] The United States Navy purchased the property in 1952 to build Oceana Master Jet Base. The Bell House is used as the residence for the commanding officer of Naval Air Station Oceana.

BROAD BAY MANOR
1710 Dey Cove Drive

Land was granted to Thomas Allen in 1655 on which a small house combining one room with a loft above, was probably built in 1660. It had brick walls eighteen inches thick.[11] The house, twenty-four feet square, was incorporated into a much larger three-story house overlooking the water.[12] Later owners included Dr. Enoch Ferebee, his son and grandson, and Dr. John B. Dey.[13]

DEWITT COTTAGE
1106 Atlantic Avenue

This cottage was built in 1895 by the first mayor of Virginia Beach, B. P. Holland. Bought by Cornelius DeWitt in 1909, it was occupied by the DeWitt family from that time until 1988, when the last of the DeWitt sisters moved to a retirement home.[14] The two-story house, which is on the Virginia Landmarks Register, has brick walls fourteen inches thick. It has twenty-two rooms, a basement and an attic. The house is the only surviving example of the typical beach house erected in Virginia Beach during its first development period, 1863-1906.[15] In 1995, after remodeling, the DeWitt Cottage opened as the Atlantic Wildfowl Heritage Museum. There are ground floor exhibits of wildfowl and hunting memorabilia.[16] The DeWitt Cottage is on the National Register of Historic Places.

FAIRFIELD

The exact site of Fairfield is unknown, but it is believed that the entrance to the house was on Kempsville Road just south of Princess Anne Road. The property extended to the south and west from there. The house was built by Anthony Walke (II), probably between 1750 and 1770. After it burned, possibly in 1865,[17] his son the Reverend David Walke, who had lived there, moved to Pleasant Hall.[18] Fairfield was an "almost baronial establishment"[19] with liveried Black servants, blacksmiths, wagon-makers, saddlers, and tradesmen imported from England. It had the appearance of a village, with a number of houses and ships.[20] The last outbuilding remaining on the property was a kitchen or possibly a coachman's house, lodge, or office. It was severely damaged by vandals in the 1970s and was torn down.[21] The Fairfield name is perpetuated by a residential community and shopping area located on the site.

FERRY FARM
4136 Cheswick Lane

William Walke built a house on this site on land devised to him by his father, Anthony Walke. The present house was built on the same foundation in the early 1800s. It was on this property that a ferry was run in 1642 by Savill Gaskin.[22] The house has been the subject of title disputes over the years.[23] The House which is on the National Register of Historic Places is owned by The City of Virginia Beach and operated as a museum.

FRANK LLOYD WRIGHT HOUSE
320 51ST Street

Designed by Frank Lloyd Wright in 1953 for Dr. and Mrs. Andrew B. Cooke, the house presents a conservative façade to the public. Away from the public view, however, the architect let the "building erupt into full geometric bloom."[24] The crescent-shaped house with a curved wall of windows created quite a stir while it was being built. Many local builders and subcontractors were unenthusiastic about the design and did not bid on the work. They were more familiar with the square Georgian designs typical in this area. Enough adventurous contractors and subcontractors were found, however, and construction proceeded. One of the most difficult problems the builders had was the steady stream of curious visitors to the site.[25]

Completed in 1959, the house is made of sand colored bricks which were manufactured in Ohio and West Virginia. Frank Lloyd Wright also designed 90 percent of the furniture, the majority of which was made locally.[26]

GREEN HILL
Lovetts Pond Road

The main house was built by Lancaster Lovett prior to 1738. A brick on the north wall is incised with the date 1738, which is thought to be the date that the roofline was raised and replaced, probably when it was owned by Lemuel Cornick. The Georgian house originally consisted of four rooms and a large cellar.[27]

Property ownership can be traced from its 1636 acquisition by Henry Southell (Southall or Southern) through the Purvine, Fulcher, Lovett, Keeling, Cornick, Godfrey, Lee, and Shull families.[28]

GREENWICH
North side of Princess Anne Road and west of Kempsville Road

This site was the location of a plantation built by William Moseley (II),[29] who married Mary Gookin, daughter of Sarah Offley Thorowgood Gookin and John Gookin. Nothing remains to indicate the exact location of this property. The names of Rolleston and Greenwich, the Moseley plantations separated by a creek, are preserved in modern developments.

KEELING HOUSE
1157 Adam Keeling Road

Thomas Keeling built this house sometime after 1680. It is a one-and-a-half story, five-bay, rectangular building and has a fine pitched "A" roof. The house is a good example of Flemish bond brickwork and has been restored to its former beauty. It has several notable features. The original woodwork includes matching cupboards on each side of the fireplace on the north wall. The house is one of only a handful of houses in Virginia which has a chevron pattern worked into the brickwork under the gables. The inverted chevron (created here in blue headers) was a distinctive late seventeenth century device.[30]

In 1683, Adam Keeling willed a 400-acre tract to his son Thomas. The property was located on the east side, near the mouth of the Lynnhaven River. It is generally accepted that the house was built after the land was transferred.[31] The Keeling House is sometimes called "Ye Dudlies." This name is probably a modern misunderstanding of an old method of shorthand. To ease the strain of writing with quill pens, words were often abbreviated. A common abbreviation for "th" was called the Thorn and looked like a "Y." Therefore, the word "ye" would have been pronounced "the" and the word "yis" was "this."[32] When Adam Keeling referred to his house at "Ye Dudlies," he may have simply been referring to the house on the former Dudley property.[33] Owned by the Keelings until 1884, the house was later owned by the Averys, Consolvos, Whites, Syers, Manesses,[34] Breedens,[35] Morgans and Carwells.[36] The Keeling House is on the National Register of Historic Places.

LAWSON HALL
Lawson Hall Road

Built by Anthony Lawson in the eighteenth century, Lawson Hall was located in the Diamond Springs area. The property became noted for its extensive boxwood gardens. In the early 1900s, a fire destroyed the house. Following the fire, a modern house was built on the site.[37] The Lawson name is perpetuated by the residential development Lawson Estates and nearby Lawson Lake, a dammed up branch of Little Creek.[38]

MASURY HOUSE
515 Wilder Drive

In 1905, Dr. John Miller Masury, heir to a paint manufacturing fortune,[39] purchased 130 acres at the beach. The acreage, which extended from Crystal Lake for a distance of one-half mile to the shore, included 800 yards of ocean frontage. The house he built was completed in 1908[40] and was the only house between 31st Street and Cape Henry. [41] It had twenty-five rooms, a ballroom, a pipe organ, an elevator, and a cedar boardwalk to the ocean.[42] There was 3,000 square feet of veranda and sun porches.[43] Electric light was generated by a private electric plant, which also powered lights for the boardwalk, a beach cottage, and an electric train which ran on Atlantic Avenue.

The three-story building, also known as "The Castle," "Greystone," or "The Wilder Place," is built of gray stone imported from Scotland. In the 1930s, the house was the Crystal Club, a casino and nightclub. It became a private residence again following World War II.[44] The Masury House is on the National Register of Historic Places.

MURRAY HOUSES

At one time there were four Murray houses, each within walking distance of the others. Two of the houses, located at the intersection of Indian River Road and Military Highway, were torn down to make room for a shopping center.[45] The other two still exist, one on either side of King's Creek.

RICHARD (or Isaac) MURRAY HOUSE
3300 Harlie Court

This brick house on the west side of King's Creek has a brick near the top of the chimney etched "I.M. 1786." The house is at least as old as the brick but probably older, as it is generally assumed to have been the first Murray family house and the site of their flax growing business.[46] Like the Thomas Murray house, this house is also laid in Flemish bond. There is a full basement with a fireplace. The house contains much original woodwork.[47]

THOMAS MURRAY HOUSE
3425 S. Crestline Drive

The Thomas Murray house is a gambrel-roofed house built of Flemish bond brick. Located on the east side of King's Creek, the house has a full basement with a fireplace. There is a center hall on the first floor. The house has wide pine floors, deep windows, and fine chimneys.[48] It is believed to have been built in 1791 by Isaac Murray for his son Thomas. Other than the installation of plumbing, electricity, and a kitchen, no modern additions have been made to this attractive house.[49] The Thomas Murray house is on the National Register of Historic Places.

PEMBROKE MANOR
320 Constitution Drive

This brick mansion was built in 1764 by the grandson of Jonathan Saunders (who was the rector of Lynnhaven Parish in 1695). At the time of the American Revolution, it was owned by the rector's great-grandson John Saunders, a Loyalist. The property escheated to the state and was bought by Captain Henry Kellam. The house is on both the Virginia Landmarks Register and the National Register of Historic Places.[50] For many years, ownership alternated among those who proposed commercial usage and those who intended historical or residential usage.[51]

PLEASANT HALL
5184 Princess Anne Road

Two bricks, set over a basement window of Pleasant Hall and inscribed with the date 1779 had long been a factor in attributing the building of the house to Peter Singleton (I), who owned it at that time. Research by Elizabeth Wingo, however, dates the construction to a period as much as a decade earlier. Using records from Virginia Beach, Richmond, and London, she identified that George Logan bought the property in 1763. Information written by George Logan's uncle, Robert Gilmour, indicated that the house was built in 1769 or 1770. Logan's widow stated in a loyalist publication of 1784 that Logan had built the house about seventeen years before.[52]

Pleasant Hall was the headquarters of Lord Dunmore following the skirmish at Kempsville. Because the owner, George Logan, sided with the British in the American Revolution, the property escheated to the state. The house, brick laid in a Flemish bond, is a fine example of Georgian architecture of the second period.[53] It has beautiful woodwork, including handsome wainscoting, elaborate cupboards and panels, and pilasters topped with Corinthian capitals.[54] So fine was the house that it was even admired by Lord Dunmore who is reported to have written, "I saw Mr. Logan's house and have never seen a better in Virginia."[55] The house is privately owned and on the National Register of Historic Places.

ROLLESTON

Rolleston was built about 1650 by William Moseley. With the exception of one brief interval, it was owned by the Moseley family for 200 years. In 1860, the property was bought by former governor Henry A. Wise. He lived there for about two years but fled when the Union army occupied the area. By 1866, Rolleston was being used by the Freedmen's Bureau. It accommodated a school and residence for former slaves, with an enrollment of 130 children and adults. The house later burned[56] and is remembered now by modern place names.

ROSE HALL
1101 Five Point Road

Jacob Ellegood built the original "Rose Hall" on this site in 1730. Many believe that the current house is similar to the frame house erected at that time. Jacob Ellegood, who was a prominent member of the community, a vestryman, and a colonel of the militia, sided with Lord Dunmore in 1775. After the Revolution, he settled in New Brunswick, Canada. A family graveyard is located on the property.[57]

TALLWOOD
1676 Kempsville Road

This house was built circa 1740 by Nathaniel Nicholas, whose grandfather arrived in Virginia in 1643. The property was owned by the Nicholas family until 1836 when it was sold to Jacob Hunter. The Hunters owned it until 1877 when it was again sold. The house is clapboard with brick at each end. The pine flooring and the stairway are original.[58]

Mrs. Lettie Gregory, who moved into the house in 1945, is credited with naming it Tallwood. The name was inspired by all of the trees which surrounded the house.[59] In recent years construction of Tallwood High School and a housing development have encircled Tallwood.

WEBLIN HOUSE
5588 Moore's Pond Road

Thomas Lambert was granted this land in 1648. John Weblin inherited it through his wife, who was Thomas Lambert's daughter. This house is believed to have been built prior to 1670. It is brick and has a large brick chimney just as the Thoroughgood house does.[60] One gable, chimney, and the rear of the house are of English bond, with the front of Flemish bond. The north gable and chimney are of a later period. Charred rafters indicate a partial burning and a later rebuilding. It is evident that the sharp roof has been altered to the gambrel roof style.[61] The Weblin House is on the National Register of Historic Places.

WOLFSNARE PLANTATION
513 West Plantation Road

This fine brick house was built in 1715 by Matthew Pallet (also spelled Pallette and Pallit). It is located on part of the Thomas Keeling grant. The house is of Flemish bond and has outside chimneys at the east and west ends.[62]

The property and house remained in the Pallett family until 1835. In the following 122 years, it had nearly one dozen owners, including the Lovitts, Hunters, and Cornicks.[63] A property development company purchased it in 1957. Although the original plans were to tear it down, the house was used as a sales office and then sold as a residence.[64] Wolfsnare Plantation is on the National Register of Historic Places.

Notes for Appendix II

1. City of Virginia Beach, Va. The Office of Research and Strategic Analysis. *City of Virginia Beach Inventory of Historic Buildings and Sites.* (Virginia Beach, Va.: City of Virginia Beach, 1990), 4-2.
2. Louisa Venable Kyle, "Bayville Survives, But Many Estates in Gay old Princess Anne are Gone," *Virginian-Pilot,* 24 May 1953, part 2, 5.
3. Louisa Venable Kyle, "Horse Racing in the Old South: How a Horse from Princess Anne County Became Champion," *Virginian-Pilot,* 15 August 1954, part 3, 5.
4. City of Virginia Beach, Va. The Office of Research and Strategic Analysis. March 1990, 4-2.
5. F. E. Turin, "The Making of a Great Port: Norfolk, Portsmouth, and Environs Today," in *Through the Years in Norfolk,* (Norfolk, Va.: n.p., 1936), 190.
6. Chris Weathersbee, "Bayville Takes Top Prizes at National Dairy Show." *Virginian-Pilot,* 30 October 1964, Beacon, 12.
7. Alex Marshall, "Bayville Farms Began in 1919 as Executive's Hobby," *Virginian-Pilot,* 17 June 1992, D5.
8. City of Virginia Beach, Va. Office of Research and Strategic Analysis. March 1990, 4-14.
9. Mary Hurst, "Commander's Residence Is Rich in History of Area," *Virginian-Pilot,* 14-15 January 1986, *Beacon,* 13.
10. City of Virginia Beach, Va. The Office of Research and Strategic Analysis. March 1990, 4-14.
11. Ibid., 4-13.
12. Louisa Venable Kyle, "Rich in Tradition, Broad Bay Manor Stands as a Reminder of More Spacious Days of Past," *Virginian-Pilot,* 22 August 1954, part 3, 3.
13. City of Virginia Beach, Va. The Office of Research and Strategic Analysis, March 1990, 4-13.
14. Marc Davis, "Old Cottage Has a Date with History," *Virginian-Pilot,* 12 April 1988, D3.
15. City of Virginia Beach, Va. The Office of Research and Strategic Analysis, March 1990, 4-43.
16. Bill Reed, "Atlantic Wildfowl Heritage Museum Has Grand Opening Saturday in the Former DeWitt Cottage," *Virginian-Pilot,* 22 September 1995, *Beacon,* 8.
17. Sadie Scott Kellam and V. Hope Kellam, *Old Houses in Princess Anne Virginia,* (Portsmouth, Va.: Printcraft, 1931), 167.
18. City of Virginia Beach, Va. The Office of Research and Strategic Analysis. March 1990, 5-3.
19. Kellam, 167.
20. Katherine Fontaine Syer, "The Town and City of Virginia Beach," in *The History of Lower Tidewater, Virginia,* vol. 2, ed. Rogers Dey Whichard (New York: Lewis Historical Publishing Company, Inc., 1959), 62.

21. Helen Crist, "Old Fairfield House to be Demolished," *The (Virginia Beach) Sun,* 17 February 1972, 1.

22. City of Virginia Beach, Va. The Office of Research and Strategic Analysis. March 1990, 4-2.

23. Greg Goldfarb, "There's a Cloud over the Title of 170-Year-Old House at the Beach," *Virginian-Pilot,* 21 February 1995, B1.

24. Sharon Young, "The Wright Angle," *Virginian-Pilot,* 14 September 1982, B1.

25. Jane Reif, "Frank Lloyd Wright Designs Unique Home for Virginia Beach," *Virginian-Pilot,* 25 October 1959, E1.

26. Sharon Young, B1.

27. City of Virginia Beach, Va. The Office of Research and Strategic Analysis. March 1990, 4-12.

28. Sadie Scott Kellam and V. Hope Kellam, *Title of Green Hill Farm Princess Anne County, Virginia.* 4 February 1932.

29. City of Virginia Beach, Va. The Office of Research and Strategic Analysis. March 1990, 5-1.

30. Ibid., 4-12.

31. Rogers Dey Whichard, *The History of Lower Tidewater Virginia,* vol. 1 (New York: Lewis Historical Publishing Company, Inc., 1959), 278.

32. Paul E. Drake, *What Did They Mean by That?: A Dictionary of Historical Terms for Genealogists* (Bowie, Md.: Heritage Books, 1994), xi.

33. Nell Kraft, "Keeling House Is a Step into the 1600's," *Virginian-Pilot,* 8 September 1977, D1.

34. Louisa Venable Kyle, "Three Long Centuries Have Huffed and Puffed But They Haven't Blown 3 Brick Houses Down," *Virginian-Pilot,* 18 January 1953, part 2, 9.

35. Nell Kraft, "Keeling House Is a Step into the 1600's," *Virginian-Pilot,* 8 September 1977, D1.

36. Patricia Neleski, "History's Mysteries Abound at the Keeling House," *Virginian-Pilot,* 5 May 2005, B8.

37. Sadie Scott Kellam and V. Hope Kellam, *Old Houses in Princess Anne Virginia* (Portsmouth, Va.: Printcraft, 1931), 219.

38. Rogers Dey Whichard, *The History of Lower Tidewater Virginia,* vol. 1 (New York: Lewis Historical Publishing Company, Inc., 1959), 279.

39. Richard Cobb, "Mansion of Your Dreams Has a Real Price," *Virginian-Pilot,* 13 February 1977, section D, part 2, 15.

40. City of Virginia Beach, Va. The Office of Research and Strategic Analyst. March 1990, 4-15.

41. Cobb, 15.

42. City of Virginia Beach, Va. The Office of Research and Strategic Analysis. March 1990, 4-15.

43. Cobb, 15.

44. City of Virginia Beach, Va. The Office of Research and Strategic Analysis. March 1990, 4-15.

45. Mary Reid Barrow, "Studying the Fate of Family Farms," *Virginian-Pilot,* 7 October 1983, *Beacon,* 6.

46. City of Virginia Beach, Va. The Office of Research and Strategic Analysis. March 1990, 4-11.

47. Mary Reid Barrow, "Growth Makes a Casualty of History," *Virginian-Pilot,* 31 July 1983, *Beacon* 6.

48. Louisa Venable Kyle, "Tuckers May Well be Proud of the Home They Have Restored for Posterity to Enjoy," *Virginian-Pilot,* 6 December 1953, part 5, 4.

49. City of Virginia Beach, Va. The Office of Research and Strategic Analysis. March 1990, 4-10.

50. Ibid., 4-1.

51. Mary Reid Barrow, "Pembroke's Historic Halls Ring with Sounds of Children," *Virginian-Pilot,* 27 October 1993, *Beacon,* 2.

52. Helen Crist, "Studies Expand Home's Historic Value," *Virginian-Pilot,* 16 April 1982, *Beacon,* 4.

53. City of Virginia Beach, Va. The Office of Research and Strategic Analysis. March 1990, 4-10.

54. Janice Dool, "Pleasant Hall Harks to Era of Revolution," *Virginian-Pilot,* 25 May 1967, *Beacon,* 12.

55. Crist, "Studies Expand Home's Historic Value," 4.

56. Stephen S. Mansfield, *Princess Anne County and Virginia Beach: A Pictorial History* (Norfolk, Va.: The Donning Company/Publishers, 1989), 66-67.

57. City of Virginia Beach, Va. The Office of Research and Strategic Analysis. March 1990, 5-6.

58. Ibid., 4-10.

59. Helen Crist, "House Gets Name from 200-Year-Old Trees," *Virginian-Pilot,* 28 March 1976, *Beacon,* 10.

60. City of Virginia Beach, Va. The Office of Research and Strategic Analysis. *City of Virginia Beach Inventory of Historic Buildings and Sites.* March 1990, 4-1.

61. Kellam and Kellam, 36.

62. City of Virginia Beach, Va. The Office of Research and Strategic Analysis. March 1990, 4-14.

63. Louisa Venable Kyle, "Around Wolf Snare Creek Villages Now Are Growing Up Belatedly, to Fulfill a Three-Century-Old Colonial Vision," *Virginian-Pilot,* 2 August 1953, part 3, 7.

64. Carol Mather, "Wolf's Snare: 263 Years Old and Brimming with Vitality," *Virginian-Pilot,* 12 September 1978, A6.

INDEX